The Future of Europe

Michael Kaeding • Johannes Pollak
Paul Schmidt
Editors

The Future of Europe

Views from the Capitals

ZukunftsFonds
der Republik Österreich

TEPSA

Co-funded by the
Europe for Citizens Programme
of the European Union

palgrave
macmillan

Editors
Michael Kaeding
University of Duisburg-Essen
Duisburg, Germany

Johannes Pollak
Webster Vienna Private University /
Institute for Advanced Studies
Vienna, Austria

Paul Schmidt
Austrian Society for European Politics
Vienna, Austria

ISBN 978-3-319-93045-9 ISBN 978-3-319-93046-6 (eBook)
https://doi.org/10.1007/978-3-319-93046-6

Library of Congress Control Number: 2018947105

Cover image: GettyImages / FrankRamspott
Cover design: Tom Howey

Printed on acid-free paper

This Palgrave Macmillan imprint is published by the registered company Springer International Publishing AG part of Springer Nature.
The registered company address is: Gewerbestrasse 11, 6330 Cham, Switzerland

Foreword

Our European history began on the islands, by the sea and on the river banks. This led the way to centuries of exchanges, a blending process where ideas, art forms and scientific endeavours nourished themselves from one another.

Merchants from Crete, craftsmen from Etruria, philosophers and playwrights from Athens, lawyers and engineers from Rome, all met and shared their ways of thinking. This dynamism unleashed by the Renaissance made us receptive to new forms of trade and to new discoveries, to finance, to manufacturing, and paved the way for the emergence of great patrons of the arts.

Through our Union, we have ushered in a new European renaissance. We have created a vast space where people can meet and exchange ideas, in which the dignity and freedom of the individual are at the heart of everything we do. We should be proud of the legacy we are passing on to our children: the freedom to travel, to study, to work, to set up a business and to innovate.

Guaranteeing freedom in the largest economic area in the world has helped us create millions of jobs. Through our cohesion policy we have worked to ensure that no-one is left behind. We need to complete this massive undertaking and exploit its untapped potential, through the digital market, the capital market and the energy market. All along, we must keep firmly in mind the cost of non-Europe, which goes well beyond an economic value.

We still believe in Europe, but we want it to work better. So many mistakes have been made. Our Union is still unfinished and it often seems remote from people's problems, divided, inefficient, and overly bureaucratic. As the President of the European Parliament, the only institution directly elected by European citizens, I am concerned at the growing disillusionment with Europe, which many of them now profess. A new start must mean bringing Europe closer to its citizens once again. This is the priority I have set for my term in office.

Window-dressing is not enough. We need far-reaching change. We need effective policies which enable us to overcome the fears of those who cannot find work, of young people who cannot see a future for themselves. We need a sound response for those who feel threatened by terrorism, by illegal immigration, and for those who are calling for us to reaffirm, loud and clear, within and beyond our borders, the values on which our Union is founded. They all call for a more practical Europe, a Europe of results.

We need to boost growth, attract investment, create jobs, make Europe fairer and more business-friendly. Our common currency must be matched by real convergence, backed by common reforms and by genuine economic governance. In addition to the Stability and Growth Pact, we need a Generational Pact. We cannot pass on unmanageable debts, and an inefficient economy hampering job creation, to our young generations. We must ensure that they too can enjoy the benefits of a social market economy. We need simpler rules and procedures. We must not get bogged down in the details of policy. Instead, we must concentrate on the major challenges facing us: foreign policy, defence, trade, climate change. In a world in which innovation and digital technologies are tearing down borders and barriers, individual States have no choice but to pool their resources. It is only by drawing on the combined power of 500 million European consumers that we can defend our interests in the world. Only in unison, can we enforce rights of ownership, and assert our safety, social, environmental and technological standards. No European State acting alone is strong enough to negotiate with the USA, China, Russia or India. Only by acting together can we exercise our sovereignty properly. We must continue to promote more open markets and put an end to unfair competition. Like our own internal market, the world market must guarantee freedom from the yoke of unnecessary regulation.

To protect our fellow citizens, we need more trust between European partners. Our intelligence services, our courts and our police forces must work together and exchange information. In the same way, if we are to monitor our borders effectively, we need a strong European Border and Coast Guard Agency. Together, standing shoulder to shoulder, we must make the right of asylum more effective by overhauling the Dublin Regulation. We must be just as rigorous in taking in people who qualify for asylum as we are in countering illegal immigration. If we are to deal with this epochal phenomenon, we need a joint strategy, which focuses on development in Africa through a robust economic diplomacy.

If we are to address these challenges properly, today more than ever we need European unity. We cannot afford to leave Europe half-finished. We need to change Europe, not destroy it. We are much more than just a market or a currency. These ideals of freedom, prosperity and peace have shaped our Union and our identity. But we must also reflect on our mistakes, and change the image of a remote, ineffectual Europe. Only in this way can we communicate to our young people that they are part of a great project once again. Let us allow them to dream once again about a better Europe and a better world.

Europe is thinking hard about its own future. We have to find answers to two fundamental questions: what it is that we want to do together in the future, and how we want to do it. The European Parliament was the first to contribute to this reflection process, through the Brok-Bresso, Böge-Bérès and Verhofstadt reports.

President Juncker has presented the Commission White Paper setting out the possible scenarios and, more recently, President Macron put on the table a range of ideas and proposals that warrant in-depth consideration.

The Conference of Presidents of the European Parliament has decided to devote a series of debates in plenary to the future of Europe, and to invite the Heads of State and Government and leading European figures who wish to speak to outline their vision and debate with us. Several Heads of State and Government have already taken the occasion to speak in the plenary of the European Parliament in Brussels and Strasbourg.

The European Parliament, the beating heart of European democracy, will respond to its institutional duty to be at the centre of this debate, and lead the way for a Europe closer to its citizens.

President of the European Parliament — Antonio Tajani
Brussels, Belgium

Why This Book?

The economic and financial turbulences of the last decade and the recent crisis of European migration policies have shaken the very foundation of European integration. These must be taken alongside the British vote to leave the European Union that triggered a reform process, which – to be successful – needs to be well on track before the United Kingdom exits the European Union (EU). The debate on the future of Europe picked up speed when Jean Claude Juncker, President of the European Commission, proposed five reform scenarios as a basis for discussion. In September 2016 at their informal meeting in Bratislava, the 27 EU heads of state and government committed to offer Europeans a vision of an attractive EU that they can trust and support. Subsequently, when commemorating the 60th anniversary of the European Union in Rome, leaders pledged to work towards a safer, stronger, and more social Europe. It is not the first time that Europeans have heard the promises of a deep reform of EU institutions, policies, and also future orientations. Will their patience be rewarded this time?

The diversity of views regarding the direction and speed of European integration seems to be getting rather bigger than smaller, as complex negotiations on the next Multiannual Financial Framework lie ahead. While some European leaders have publicly reiterated their European preferences, others have preferred to issue statements jointly and, further, others have remained silent. However, it was the European lecture by French president Emmanuel Macron at the Sorbonne University in Paris that revived and drew the most of public attention. While the European Commission has already been organizing citizen's dialogues all over

Europe for quite a while, the French president was the first national leader to call for democratic assemblies on the future of Europe to be held in every EU-country before the next elections to the European Parliament in 2019. This public call was crucial because Macron, addressing his fellow colleagues, touched on one of the weak spots of European integration: the lack of national political ownership and public debates. The debate on the future of Europe needs to reach all member states to gain momentum, and it needs to engage with Europeans on all levels possible.

This book sheds light on the political dynamics within the EU member states and contributes to the national discussions about Europe. We have asked authors from the – still – 28 member states as well as Iceland, Switzerland, Norway, and Turkey to assess in short, concise, and easy-to-read opinion pieces how their respective country could get more involved in the European debate. They take the reader on a journey through various political landscapes and different views. In the end, they all have one thing in common: they want national politics to finally get involved in shaping the European project.

The manifold contributions reflect the diversity of Europe. The articles cover issues ranging from a perceived lack of ambition at the periphery to a careful balancing act between diverse national players and their standpoints at the geographical centre. The future of Europe is not only about bridging the dividing policy lines, but it is also about shifting powers, regaining trust and support for the European integration process, and the need to create policies that work. In the end, nobody is born a Eurosceptic.

Yet, discussions share common features: the anxiety regarding national sovereignty and the reflection on the division of power in Europe, the different levels of political activism to defend one's interests, the migration and border discourse, as well as security concerns, among other examples.

The opinion pieces on countries with an external border, such as Italy, Malta, Bulgaria, Greece, the Baltic States, and Finland have, as one might expect, a particular focus on the security dimension of the Union as well as the migration challenge. For example, due to the worsening security environment, Finland is a frontrunner in arguing for a deepened defence cooperation, mutual assistance, and solidarity. On the other hand, Malta, as a small state that benefits from the EU's policies in many fields, could contribute through its established links with Northern African states. Recent events have transformed public opinion in Italy, a country that has moved from a deep love for the EU to severe dissatisfaction. The further evolution of this relationship will depend very much on the answers given to the two most sensible issues for the Italian public: economic growth and migration control.

In respect to the latter, the authors of the Slovak piece, as well as those of other CEE countries, encourage their governments to bring more realism into the debate and look at the real numbers as opposed to escalating rhetoric and evoking the "fear of the others".

The writers from Lithuania and Latvia point to the level of emigration of young people – a brain drain challenge with which many central, southern and eastern EU member states are confronted. At the same time, Estonia has become a hub for digital innovation by turning itself into a pathfinder for e-solutions. Thus, in a small geographical space, we find trends and countertrends that very much highlight the success and challenges national governments face.

Due to the legal and political frictions with the EU, the authors from Hungary and Poland emphasize the importance of the EU's credibility, which they see is at stake. They urgently call for a clear and firm EU position regarding the application of its own norms and values. Yes, migration and the economy are issues, but where would Europe's post World War II claim to humanity, enlightenment, and equality stand if reactionary identity politics would creep back in at the expense of the weakest in our societies?

The contributions on France, Belgium, Luxembourg, and Ireland argue for a multispeed Europe. For Macron's vision of Europe, there are no red lines but new horizons. But do his plans really appeal to blue collar workers? Here, the authors suggest that a European unemployment scheme could be of assistance. Belgium, on the other hand, is described as a former custodian of the European integration process. Today, however, its proactivity is disappearing due to its internal political constitution. In Luxembourg, again, support for integration occasionally goes even beyond pure cost-benefit calculations through, for example, demands for a stronger social pillar. Still, the author describes certain preferences for a multispeed Europe to overcome current tensions between the member states. For Dublin, in turn, the UK's decision to leave the EU changes everything. Thus, a recalibration of its European strategy is deemed necessary to strike a new balance between proactive European engagement as a core member of the European Union and the preservation of its distinctive national interests, e.g. military neutrality and tax competition.

The pieces from Austria and Slovenia argue that their countries should focus and prioritize in order to be heard and make a difference. Both could become much more active EU members if they carefully choose the policy areas in which they can bring value added to the European discussion. This calls for an open screening process at home and an honest evaluation of each country's potential. Austria considers itself a bridge builder between central, eastern and western Europe. In order to put their money where their mouth is, Austria should invest more in sustainable strategic alliances.

The articles on Romania and Bulgaria draw on the country's experiences regarding EU-enlargement. In addition, they consider their countries as laboratories of political trends that are common for the whole of Europe, like the rise of populism or nationalistic conservatism.

Portugal and Spain take the approach of the "good pupil": two countries committed to the European integration process despite moderate criticism that have not really had a clear strategy towards EU integration since their accession. This highlights a common feature of the integration process as such: once a state secures membership in the club, further development of the club takes a backseat. Or even worse, membership in the club is downplayed and used for petty domestic politics – the place where political power and office are still predominantly traded.

Sweden, Denmark, Croatia, and the Czech Republic are perceived as outliers, as each tries to find their way through managing the risk of belonging to the periphery of integration. Denmark is occupying a peculiar position due to its many opt-outs, and it creates a special environment for those who want to move ahead and deepen the Union: it is an environment where those who fear being isolated determine the speed of integration. Thus, if it wants to be heard, it is advised to stay close to the core, sometimes even circumventing the exemptions. The Swedish government is also reminded that its preference for the status quo might not be sufficient to decisively influence the debate. For their part, the Czechs' negative views on the EU are largely a result of the perceived political disconnect between domestic concerns and broader EU-related issues. But if worries about e.g. East-West double food standards, fair taxation, and the protection of the external borders of the EU were to be overcome, the country is seen to have the potential to become an active member state with a clear defined agenda again. On the other hand, Croatia's primary goal as the youngest EU member remains full accession to the EU, i.e. joining the Schengen area and the eurozone. A more integrated Croatia could also be a significant gain for the future enlargement process of other south eastern European countries.

Iceland, Norway, Switzerland, and Turkey, on their part, assess the different ways to adhere to and influence EU decision making without being members of the Union, which also provide potential lessons for the UK in its search for an adequate future relationship with the EU. Iceland, for example, is advised to increase its weight in Europe through a three-fold strategy: team up its European expertise at home, deepen the Iceland-German alliance, and establish closer relations with the Nordic states on European affairs.

Clearly, the future of Europe is not an academic debate! There is an obvious need to talk about Europe more vigorously in all capitals and every corner of Europe because this is where its future will be decided. Governments have to spearhead those deliberations not by drawing red lines, but by engaging as many people as possible to gauge the future direction of Europe. Public support depends on whether the benefits of European integration outweigh any negative effects on respective national interests. Citizens′ views are as diverse as they are exciting. Ultimately, Europe needs all the support it can muster. Governments' tasks are to foster debate, listen, and then make a new Europe possible.

We would like to thank Christoph Breinschmid for the editorial processing and his tireless efforts to make this project happen.

Michael Kaeding
Johannes Pollak
Paul Schmidt

Contents

Austria in Europe: Size Matters: But so Do Ideas 1
Paul Schmidt

Belgium in Search of a Stance on Today's EU Integration Dilemmas 5
Nathalie Brack and Amandine Crespy

Bulgaria: More Europe in Domestic Politics 9
Daniel Smilov

Croatia: Finally in the EU but Still in Search for a Place Under the (EU) Sun 13
Jakša Puljiz

A Future Europe for Cyprus: A Struggle to Overcome the Utopianism of the 1990s and Come to Terms with the Tough Pragmatism of the 2020s 17
Giorgos Kentas

Czech Republic: A Paradise for Eurosceptics? 21
Petr Kratochvíl and Zdeněk Sychra

The Schizophrenic Danes 25
Marlene Wind

Has the Estonian e-Tiger Been Caught Napping? 29
Viljar Veebel

Bridging the EU's Political Dividing Lines Is in Finland's Security Interest 33
Juha Jokela

France: Supporting the Jobless – A Job for Europe 37
Xavier Ragot and Olivier Rozenberg

Germany and the EU: Managing Differentiation to Avoid Structural Segregation 41
Andreas Maurer

Greece: Of "Future of Europe" Plans and Political Honesty 45
Xenophon Yataganas and A. D. Papagiannidis

Hungary: Becoming Pioneers Again 49
Péter Balázs

Active Participation, an Icelandic-German Alliance and United Nordic Front 53
Baldur Thorhallsson

Ireland and the EU: A Pragmatic Approach to Integration 57
Cian McCarthy

Italy and the EU: A Relationship with Uncertain Outcomes 61
Sergio Fabbrini

Latvia's Future in a Deepened EU: Fine with the Right Wine 65
Karlis Bukovskis and Aldis Austers

Lithuania and the EU: Pragmatic Support Driven by Security Concerns 69
Ramūnas Vilpišauskas

Luxembourg and the EU: How to Integrate in the Face of Diversity 73
Anna-Lena Högenauer

Malta: Small and Peripheral but Aiming for the Core of Europe 77
Mark Harwood

The Netherlands and the EU: Strengthening but Not Centralising the EU 81
Adriaan Schout

Exit, Voice, and Loyalty: Norway's Options 85
Ulf Sverdrup

Solidarity with Poland but Not from Poland 89
Zdzisław Mach

The Bell Has Rung: Portugal's Main Bet Is on the Conclusion of the EMU 93
Alice Cunha

The EU's Young and Restless Democracy: Romania's Lessons and Contribution 97
Bianca Toma

Being European: The Slovak Way 101
Ol'ga Gyárfášová and Lucia Mokrá

Slovenia: From High Enthusiasm to Frustrating Indifference 105
Maja Bučar

Spain in the EU: Eager to Regain Centrality 109
Ignacio Molina

Managing the Risk of Periphery: Sweden and the Future of the EU 113
Göran von Sydow

Towards a "Reset" of EU-Swiss Relations? 117
Frank Schimmelfennig

Like a Candle in the Wind? Insights and Recommendations on the Turkish Accession to the EU 121
Başak Alpan

The Union after Brexit: Disintegration, Differentiation or Deepening? 125
Brendan Donnelly

Index 129

Notes on Contributors

Başak Alpan is an Associate Professor and a Lecturer in European Politics and Political Sociology at the Centre for European Studies and the Department of Political Science and Public Administration at the Middle East Technical University, Ankara, Turkey. She conducts research and extensively writes on European integration, discourse theory, post structuralism, Turkish-EU relations, and football and identity.

The Centre for European Studies of the Middle East Technical University in Ankara, Turkey was founded in 1997. It aims to contribute to comparative research on Europe and European integration through an interdisciplinary team of researchers. Through the teaching and research strengths of four academic departments at METU (International Relations, Political Science and Public Administration, Economics and Business Administration), it offers two different Master of Science programmes in European Studies and European Integration. CES-METU became a Jean Monnet Centre of Excellence in 2007.

Aldis Austers is a researcher at LIIA and a visiting lecturer at Riga Stradins University. His fields of interest include monetary economics, political economy, migration, and EU integration.

The Latvian Institute of International Affairs (LIIA) was established in May 1992 in Riga as a non-profit foundation charged with the task of providing Latvia's decision-makers, experts, and the wider public with analysis, recommendations, and information about international developments, regional security issues, and foreign policy strategy and choices. It is an independent research institute that conducts research, develops publications, and organizes lectures, seminars, and conferences related to international affairs.

Péter Balázs is the Director of the Center for European Neighborhood Studies (CENS) at Central European University (CEU) in Budapest. In 2009–2010, he was the Foreign Minister of Hungary. He was also a State Secretary for Industry and Trade (1992–1993) and a State Secretary for European Integration (2002–2003). He was nominated to be the Ambassador of Hungary to Denmark (1994–1996), Germany (1997–2000), and to the EU in Brussels (2003–2004) and acquired experience in various EU positions. He was the first Hungarian member of the European Commission in 2004.

The Center for European Neighborhood Studies (CENS) was founded in 2005 as an institution of advanced research into the EU enlargement process. The overall goal of the Center is to promote a dialogue between member states and partners in eastern and southern Europe, academics, and decision makers in the EU and in national governments so that they may have a more informed understanding of factors that influence Europe's common future.

Nathalie Brack is an Assistant Professor in Political Science and European Studies at the Université Libre de Bruxelles (Cevipol – ULB) and a Visiting Professor at the College of Europe (Bruges). Over the past few years, she has been a visiting fellow at Oxford University, Sciences Po Bordeaux, and the University of Antwerp and a Visiting Professor at the University of Lausanne and the Université Catholique de Louvain. Her research interests include Euroscepticism, radical parties, political representation, and the linkage between citizens and elites. She recently authored *Opposing Europe in the European Parliament. Rebels and Radicals in the Chamber* (2018, Palgrave) and co-authored *How the EU really works* (forthcoming, Routledge).

The Institute for European Studies of the Université Libre de Bruxelles has asserted itself as a key player in the four areas of research, education, European public debate, and international relations since its foundation in 1963. It has earned the Institute the distinction of being a Jean Monnet centre of excellence. In 2009–2010, it hosted some 280 students, since its founding nearly 5000 students have graduated from the institution.

Maja Bučar is a Professor at the Faculty of Social Sciences at the University of Ljubljana. She is also the Head of the Centre of International Relations, a TEPSA member. Her research mainly focuses on international development cooperation and S&T policies, but also on EU policies and Slovenia's role in international relations.

The Centre of International Relations is a research unit within the Faculty of Social Sciences at the University of Ljubljana. The Centre conducts interdisciplinary research in the fields of international relations, international economics and international business, politics of international law, diplomacy and human rights, international organisations, and European integration.

Karlis Bukovskis is the Deputy Director of the Latvian Institute for International Affairs (LIIA) and a visiting lecturer on global political economy, international financial system, and the EU integration at Riga Graduate School of Law and Riga Stradins University.

The Latvian Institute of International Affairs (LIIA) was established in May 1992 in Riga as a non-profit foundation charged with the task of providing Latvia's decision-makers, experts, and the wider public with analysis, recommendations, and information about international developments, regional security issues, and foreign policy strategy and choices. It is an independent research institute that conducts research, develops publications, and organizes lectures, seminars, and conferences related to international affairs.

Amandine Crespy is a Lecturer of Political Science and European Studies at the Université Libre de Bruxelles (ULB) and the College of Europe (Bruges). Over the past few years, she was invited to be a visiting fellow at Sciences Po in Paris, Harvard University, the London School of Economics, Queen Mary University of London, and the Universiteit van Amsterdam. Her research deals with the politicisation of EU integration and socio-economic policies. She has a special interest in the role of ideas, discourse, and conflict in relation to democracy in Europe. Aside from her numerous publications in highly profiled international journals, she co-edited *Social Policy and the Eurocrisis* (Palgrave, 2015) and authored *Welfare Markets in Europe. The democratic challenge of European Integration* (Palgrave, 2016).

The Institute for European Studies of the Université Libre de Bruxelles has asserted itself as a key player in the four areas of research, education, European public debate, and international relations since its foundation in

1963. It has earned the Institute the distinction of being a Jean Monnet centre of excellence. In 2009–2010, it hosted some 280 students, since its founding nearly 5000 students have graduated from the institution.

Alice Cunha is a Research Fellow at the Institute of Contemporary History – NOVA University, where she is also the Co-Coordinator of the research line on European Integration History. She is the author of several publications, most of them related to Portugal and European integration.

The Institute of Contemporary History is a research centre that covers a broad range of topics under the modern and contemporary history fields.

Brendan Donnelly has been Director of the Federal Trust since January 2003. He is a former Member of the European Parliament (1994–1999). He was educated at Oxford, after which he worked in the Foreign Office, the European Parliament, and the European Commission.

The Federal Trust is a research institute studying the interactions between regional, national, European, and global levels of government. Founded in 1945 on the initiative of Sir William Beveridge, it has long made a powerful contribution to the study of federalism and federal systems. It has always had a particular interest in the European Union and Britain's place in it. The Federal Trust has no allegiance to any political party. It is registered as a charity for the purposes of education and research.

Sergio Fabbrini is the Director of the School of Government and a Professor of Political Science and International Relations at the LUISS Guido Carli University in Rome, where he holds a Jean Monnet Chair. His latest book is *Which European Union? Europe After the Euro Crisis* (Cambridge University Press, 2015).

The School of Government is part of Libera Università Internazionale degli Studi Sociali (LUISS) Guido Carli, a multidisciplinary University offering degrees at all academic levels. The focus is on business studies, economics, politics, and law. The campus is located in the centre of Rome and presents a modern study environment for 7000 students.

Ol'ga Gyarfášová is the Head of the Institute of European Studies and International Relations at Faculty of Social and Economic Sciences, Comenius University (FSES CU) in Bratislava. Her research focuses on electoral studies, political culture, public opinion, minority rights, and gender studies, as well as on analyses of populism and right-wing extremism.

The Institute of European Studies and International Relations is an integral part of the FSES CU. It is the leading higher educational institution in the areas of European Studies and Political Science in Slovakia. The Institute's research mainly focuses on the following topics: European institutions, EU policies, international organisations and international relations, political philosophy, political sociology, and political communication. Before joining the Institute, members served as experts and advisors for the ministries and contributed to the development of strategic documents in the area of international and European affairs.

Mark Harwood is the Director of the Institute for European Studies at the University of Malta. He previously worked for the European Commission and the Maltese Government. His specialisation is on the impact of the EU on Maltese politics as well as EU lobbying.

The Institute for European Studies, founded in 1991, is a teaching and research institute at the University of Malta. Offering a full range of degree programmes from undergraduate to doctoral degrees, the Institute has an alumni network of 700.

Anna-Lena Högenauer is a Senior Researcher at the University of Luxembourg. She has studied at the University of Edinburgh, the College of Europe and King's College London.

Political science at the University of Luxembourg focuses predominantly on European governance. It focuses, in particular, on multilevel governance and democracy, political economy, and education policy.

Juha Jokela is the Director of the European Union research programme at FIIA. The programme focuses on the EU's foreign and security policy and major trends in European integration. Previously, he has worked in research functions in the EU Institute for Security Studies, the Ministry for Foreign Affairs of Finland, and the University of Helsinki. He is a member of the TEPSA Board.

The Finnish Institute of International Affairs is a research institute whose mission is to produce high quality, topical information on international relations and the EU. The Institute realizes its aims by conducting research, organizing domestic and international seminars, and publishing reports on its research and current international issues.

Michael Kaeding is Professor of European Integration and European Union Politics at the Institute of Political Science of the University of Duisburg-Essen, Germany. He is a visiting fellow at the European Institute of Public Administration (EIPA) in Maastricht and guest lectures at the College of Europe, Bruges, and the German-Turkish University in Istanbul. He is chairman of TEPSA (Trans European Policy Accosiation) and leads the H2020 project SEnECA dealing with the strengthening and energizing of EU–Central Asia relations. His academic research covers books and articles on non-voters at European elections; the micromanagement of European institutions; European agencies; implementation of EU legislation, norms and values in member states; and forms of classic and alternative EU decision-making (delegated acts and comitology).

Giorgos Kentas is an Associate Professor of International Politics and Governance at the University of Nicosia and the Director of the Graduate Programme in Public Administration. He is also a Policy Advisor at the Center for Sustainable Peace and Democratic Development (SeeD).

The Center for European and International Affairs at the University of Nicosia was founded in March 1993 as an independent, non-profit institution. It seeks to advance academic and policy-oriented research and to contribute to the study and analysis of important economic, political, and social issues revolving around Cyprus, the Eastern Mediterranean, the EU, and the international environment.

Petr Kratochvíl is the Director of the Institute of International Relations in Prague and a Member of the TEPSA Board. He also serves as the Chairman of the Academic Board of Czech MFA's Diplomatic Academy. The author of dozens of monographs, book chapters, and journal articles, his research interests cover theories of international relations, European studies, and the religion-politics nexus.

The Institute of International Relations (IIR) is an independent public research institution which has been conducting scholarly research in the area of international relations since 1957. The Ministry of Foreign Affairs of the Czech Republic founded the institution. IIR tries to form a link between the academic world, the public, and international political practice.

Zdzisław Mach is a Professor of Sociology, Social Anthropology, and European Studies at the Jagiellonian University in Kraków, Poland. He is also the founder of the Institute for European Studies at the Jagiellonian University and one of the main authors of the European Studies curriculum in Poland. He is the UNESCO Chair for Education about the Holocaust and the Dean of the Faculty of International and Political Studies at the Jagiellonian University. His research interests cover issues such as nationalism, minorities and ethnicity, the development of European citizenship, migration, cultural construction of identities, collective memory, and cultural heritage as well as the development of the idea of Europe.

The Institute for European Studies is a part of the Faculty of International and Political Studies at Jagiellonian University – the oldest and the leading university in Poland. The Institute is famous for its interdisciplinary approach that combines the perspectives of anthropology, economy, cultural studies, political sciences, history, law, and sociology.

Andreas Maurer is a Professor and the Jean Monnet Chair for Political Science and European Integration Studies at the University of Innsbruck and a Senior Fellow of the German Institute for International and Security Affairs (SWP), Berlin. He studied Political Science, European and International Public Law, Sociology, and Sociopsychology at the University of Frankfurt/Main, University Aix/Marseille, the College of Europe, Bruges, and the University of Giessen. His research concentrates on multi-level parliamentarism, the EU's trade policy, and interinstitutional dynamics within the EU.

The German Institute for International and Security Affairs (Stiftung Wissenschaft und Politik, SWP) advises political decision-makers on international politics and foreign and security policy. Their services are orientated primarily towards the German government and Bundestag, as well as relevant international organisations such as the European Union, NATO and the United Nations.

Cian McCarthy is a Researcher at the Institute of International and European Affairs (IIEA). He coordinates the IIEA's programme on the Future of the EU27 and the European Perspectives forum.

The Institute of International and European Affairs is Ireland's leading think tank on European and international affairs. Its aim is to provide a forum for those with an interest in strategic planning in Irish foreign and EU policy and to evaluate and disseminate strategic policy options in these areas.

Lucia Mokrá is the Dean of FSES CU and an Associate Professor of International and European Law. Her expertise is on international law, European law, European institutions, EU foreign policy, and human rights. She is also Rapporteur of the Intergovernmental Council of the UNESCO MOST programme and a Board Member of TEPSA.

The Institute of European Studies and International Relations is an integral part of the FSES CU. It is the leading higher educational institution in the areas of European Studies and Political Science in Slovakia. The Institute's research mainly focuses on the following topics: European institutions, EU policies, international organisations and international relations, political philosophy, political sociology, and political communication. Before joining the Institute, members served as experts and advisors for the ministries and contributed to the development of strategic documents in the area of international and European affairs.

Ignacio Molina is a Senior Analyst at the Elcano Royal Institute and a Lecturer at the Department of Politics and International Relations at the Universidad Autónoma de Madrid. His areas of interest and expertise include the foreign and EU policies of Spain, the future of the European Union, and the Europeanisation of Spain's politics and government.

The Elcano Royal Institute is the leading Spanish think tank on international affairs and strategic studies. It aims to analyse world and EU events or trends from Spanish, European, and global perspectives. The Institute was established in 2001 as a private foundation under the honorary presidency of H.M. the King.

A. D. Papagiannidis is a Journalist, an Attorney at Law, and the Academic Director at EKEME/EPLO.

The Greek Centre of European Studies and Research (EKEME in its Greek acronym) was founded in 1980 by a group of academics, legal practitioners, economists, and social scientists. It operates as a non-profit institution independent of any political or state affiliation. EKEME has worked to shed light on several aspects of Greece's membership to the EC/EU and to its integration process with facts, studies, and research programs, through participation in transnational research ventures.

Johannes Pollak is the Director of and a Professor of Political Science at the Webster Vienna Private University. He is also a Senior Research fellow at the Institute for Advanced Studies, Vienna (currently on leave) and a Lecturer at the Universities of Salzburg and Vienna.

Founded in the U.S. in 1915, Webster University is an American university with a global perspective. The Vienna Campus, Webster Vienna Private University, opened in 1981 and is accredited both in the USA and in Austria.

As an independent post-university research center the Institute for Advanced Studies is well-established and recognized across Europe. The Institute develops research questions in dialogue with policy-makers as well as the academic world, and delivers answers that are relevant to both sides.

Jakša Puljiz is the Head of Department for European Integration at the Institute for Development and International Relations in Zagreb, a former Economic Advisor to the Prime Minister, and a former Deputy Minister at the Ministry of Regional Development and EU Funds.

The Institute for Development and International Relations (IRMO) is a public research institute that deals with international economic, political, and cultural relations important to the Republic of Croatia. It is focused on the European Union and the impact of EU policies in the national context.

Xavier Ragot is the President of the OFCE (Observatoire français des conjonctures économiques / French Economic Observatory), a Professor at the Department of Economics at Sciences Po, and the Director of Research at the CNRS (Centre national de la recherche scientifique / National Center for Scientific Research).

The National Center for Scientific Research, or CNRS, is a public organization under the responsibility of the French Ministry of Education and Research.

The Paris-based Observatoire français des conjonctures économiques (OFCE), or French Economic Observatory, is an independent and publicly-funded centre whose activities focus on economic research, forecasting, and evaluating public policy.

Olivier Rozenberg is an Associate Professor at Sciences Po in the Centre d'études européennes et de politiques comparées (CEE). His research focuses mainly on political institutions, parliaments and legislators, Europeanization, and the sociology of legislators.

Sciences Po is the leading French research university in political science, international relations, and sociology, according to the recently published QS rankings of international universities by discipline. The CEE is a research centre founded at Sciences Po in 2005 to fulfil three main missions: to develop research on European questions at Sciences Po, to facilitate Sciences Po's insertion in European research networks, and to foster the European debate on the future of Europe. It is also a member of the Trans European Policy Studies Association (TEPSA).

Frank Schimmelfennig is a Professor of European Politics and a member of the Centre for Comparative and International Studies. His main research interest lies in the theory of European integration and, more specifically, in EU enlargement, differentiated integration, democracy promotion, and democratization.

The Centre for Comparative and International Studies (CIS) brings together the Governance Section of ETH Zürich and the Institute of Political Science at the University of Zürich. Its European Politics (EUP) research group conducts research on European integration that focuses on the institutional development, politics, and policy-making of the European Union.

Paul Schmidt has been the Secretary General of the Austrian Society for European Politics since 2009. Previously, he worked at the Oesterreichische Nationalbank, both in Vienna and at their Representative Office in Brussels at the Permanent Representation of Austria to the European Union. His current work mainly focuses on the analysis and discussion of topical issues regarding European integration. Paul's comments and op-eds are regularly published in Austrian as well as international media.

The Austrian Society for European Politics (Österreichische Gesellschaft für Europapolitik, ÖGfE) was founded in 1991 and aims to promote and support communication on European affairs in Austria. With its headquarters in Vienna, the Society is a non-governmental and non-partisan platform mainly constituted by the Austrian Social Partners and the Oesterreichische Nationalbank.

Adriaan Schout is Senior Research Fellow and Coordinator Europe. He combines research and consultancy on European governance questions for national and European institutions. He has worked on projects addressing issues of the EU presidency, EU integration, and improving EU regulation, amongst others. His work includes *The coordination of European Governance: exploring the capacities for networked governance* (Oxford University Press, 2006), which was written alongside Andrew Jordan and resulted in the prize for 'Best Book in Contemporary European Integration Studies' from University Association for Contemporary European Studies (UACES), publisher of *the Journal of Common Market Studies*.

The Clingendael Institute is an independent think tank and diplomatic academy that conducts research and trainings for governments, civil society, and the private sector. Clingendael publishes reports, policy briefs, and short analyses and offers a wide spectrum of training programmes. As an independent platform, the Institute organises policy exchanges, conferences, and roundtables aimed at enhancing the quality of debate about international affairs. Clingendael works on international security, European affairs, conflict management, sustainability, and geostrategic analysis.

Daniel Smilov is a comparative constitutional lawyer and political scientist. He is the Programme Director at the Sofia-based Centre for Liberal Strategies, an Associate Professor of Political Theory at the University of Sofia, and a Recurrent Visiting Professor of Comparative Constitutional Law at Central European University in Budapest.

The Centre for Liberal Strategies was created in 1994 as an independent non-governmental organization. The research activities of CLS pursue academic depth while reacting to current problems in political, economic, and social life in Bulgaria and taking into account the context of today's global world. The analytical work of CLS covers national, regional, and global issues. As one of Bulgaria's primary think tanks, CLS is actively involved in structuring and implementing the public debate in the country on key issues.

Ulf Sverdrup is the Director of the Norwegian Institute of International Affairs (NUPI). Before taking up the position at NUPI, he was a Professor at the Norwegian Business School BI and a Research Professor at ARENA, Centre for European Studies at the University of Oslo.

NUPI has been a leading community for research and communication about international affairs of relevance for Norway for more than 50 years.

Zdeněk Sychra works at the Department of International Relations and European Studies at Masaryk University in Brno. He focuses on analyzing European and EU politics, especially on the Economic and Monetary Union and the horizontal integration of the EU.

The Department of International Relations and European Studies at the Faculty of Social Studies at Masaryk University was founded in 2002 as an academic institution offering education at the European level in the field of international territorial studies.

Göran von Sydow is the Deputy Director and a Senior Researcher in political science at the Swedish Institute for European Policy Studies (SIEPS). His main research interests are political parties, Euroscepticism, European integration, and constitutional change.

The Swedish Institute for European Policy Studies, SIEPS, is an independent government agency that conducts and promotes research and analysis of European policy affairs. SIEPS strives to act as a link between the academic world and policy-makers at various levels.

Baldur Thorhallsson is the Head of and a Professor at the Faculty of Political Science at the University of Iceland. He is also the Jean Monnet Chair in European Studies and the Programme and Research Director at the Centre for Small States at the University. His research focuses primarily on small state studies, European integration, and Iceland's foreign policy.

The Institute of International Affairs (IIA) is a research, teaching, and service institute in the field of international relations and European integration at the University of Iceland. Three Centres are run under the auspices of the IIA: The Jean Monnet Centre of Excellence – the Centre of Small State Studies, the Centre for Arctic Policy Studies, and Höfði the Reykjavík Peace Centre.

Bianca Toma is the Programs Director with the Romanian Centre for European Policies (CRPE) and a former EU Affairs correspondent for the mainstream media.

Founded in 2009, CRPE is one of the most experienced regional think tanks based in Bucharest and Chisinau. CRPE's mission is to promote Romania as an influential player in the development of the agenda and policies of the European Union.

Viljar Veebel is a researcher and consultant who works at the University of Tartu, The Estonian School of Diplomacy, The Tallinn Technological University, and the Estonian Foreign Policy Institute. Since 2013, he has also worked in the Estonian National Defense Academy as an Associate Professor of Social Sciences. Furthermore, Viljar Veebel is actively participating as a consultant in European Union related projects in Moldova, Georgia, Ukraine, and the Balkan area.

The Estonian Foreign Policy Institute (Eesti Välispoliitika Instituut – EVI) was founded in 2000. It is an independent think tank that is primarily funded by the Estonian Ministry of Foreign Affairs. EVI's mission is to promote a deeper understanding of international affairs and of Estonia's role in a changing world by providing a forum for informed discussion, analysis, and debate.

Ramūnas Vilpišauskas is the Director of and a Professor at the Institute of International Relations and Political Science (IIRPS), Vilnius University. Between 2004 and 2009, he worked as the Chief Economic Policy Advisor to the President of Lithuania, Valdas Adamkus, and as the Head of the Economics and Social Policy Group. He has also been the chief of staff to the President (2006–2009). His main research interests include the political economy of European integration, policy analysis of public sector reforms, and international political economy. He has been a visiting fellow at several universities in the USA and Canada and a Fulbright scholar at the Columbia University. He also conducted research at a number of European institutions including the European University Institute (Florence).

IIRPS is part of Vilnius University, which offers the most popular political science study programs in Lithuania and conducts research in international relations and political science areas including European studies. Its researchers have published extensively on the subjects of European integration and provided policy advice to Lithuanian institutions.

Marlene Wind is a Professor and the Director of the Centre for European Politics (CEP) and a Professor of Law at iCourts Centre of Excellence and the Faculty of Law, both at the University of Copenhagen. Her research is, among other things, focused on the institutional changes and treaties of the European Union, including Danish EU policymaking and Danish opt-outs. In recent years, her research emphasis has been on the interplay between law and politics in the European Union but also on politics and law from a more theoretical point of view.

The Centre for European Politics (CEP) is a research centre at the Department of Political Science at the University of Copenhagen. The centre was established in October 2007 and concerns itself with research within the field of European politics, particularly on the European Union.

Xenophon Yataganas is a current Associate Professor at the Law School (Athens University), a former Legal Advisor of the European Commission, and a member of the EKEME Curatorium (European Public Law Organization, EPLO).

The Greek Centre of European Studies and Research (EKEME in its Greek acronym) was founded in 1980 by a group of academics, legal practitioners, economists, and social scientists. It operates as a non-profit institution independent of any political or state affiliation. EKEME has worked to shed light on several aspects of Greece's membership to the EC/EU and to its integration process with facts, studies, and research programs, through participation in transnational research ventures.

Austria in Europe: Size Matters: But so Do Ideas

Paul Schmidt

In recent years, European policy initiatives from Vienna were rather unusual. Austria regularly emphasized its anti-nuclear policy stance, made the case for a stronger social dimension of the Union by championing efforts to tackle youth unemployment and questioning distortions related to the free movement of people and services, cooperated with its neighbours to fight illegal migration, and was resistant to economic and free trade agreements such as CETA and TTIP. Similar to other countries, discourse regarding the EU in Austria has always been very much determined by public sentiment at home. While defending a proactive European standpoint is still perceived to be risky business, a reality-check on national sovereignty is regularly declined. Yet, Austria has participated in practically all steps of European integration. The country rightly considers itself to be part of Europe's core and shows increasing approval rates for EU membership despite years of scepticism. However, ambition does not always match reality. The gaps between self-perception, action, and inertia provide for a "peculiar melange".

P. Schmidt (✉)
Austrian Society for European Politics, Vienna, Austria
e-mail: paul.schmidt@oegfe.at

M. Kaeding et al. (eds.), *The Future of Europe*,
https://doi.org/10.1007/978-3-319-93046-6_1

Austria awoke from its complacent regard of EU affairs during the migration challenge. Since late summer 2015, when one million people transited the country, politicians have been painfully stressing their diligent actions to control the situation, which in fact they never lost. At present, Austria accommodates approximately 150.000 refugees, which is more than those accommodated by Germany per capita. The integration process remains a crucial question. The political discourse, however, is mainly concentrated on security, justice, and identity and on the apparent inaction of the EU to protect the integrity of its borders. The same holds true for intra-EU migration, where political messages mainly focus on access to social benefits, wage dumping, and distorted competition. Worker postings in Austria and family allowances to children raised in another member state are hotly debated topics. Once again, it seems that national concerns trump the ability to find European solutions.

With a new government of conservatives and the EU-sceptic far-right Freedom Party in office, these topics have gained further momentum. The current Austrian chancellor faces the challenge to reconcile the pro-European, but rather defensive, position of the government with the undeniable fact that his coalition partner forms part of a radically populistic anti-EU group in the European Parliament.

When it comes to the future of European integration, the Austrian government eyes the concept of a social union with scepticism and is careful not to increase a post-Brexit EU-budget by arguing for a more effective and subsidiary Union. It, thus, wants to see the EU doing "less, but more efficiently". Due to its geographical proximity and historical close relations, Vienna supports the EU enlargement path of the Western Balkan countries. Concerning Turkey, however, Austria pushes for a bespoke partnership with Ankara instead of full membership. In regards to the energy sector, Austria seeks advancements on the EU level and continues its support for renewable energy policies. Despite being a neutral country, Austria would like to see more cooperation in the areas of security and defence. However, it is difficult to discern more than those rather general headers. Concrete examples and policy initiatives are hard to come by.

To foster the country's influence and exhibit a constructive approach towards EU concerns, Austria could reflect upon the following elements:

If the country wants to have a say in the future design of the EU, it needs to be clear about its priorities, respond to the pertinent ideas on the table, and propose concrete solutions. In this context, Austria would be well advised to build sustainable strategic alliances with other EU member states rather than look for ad hoc coalitions on issues of interest. The fact that a city like Vienna, ranked regularly among the three capitals with the highest quality of living worldwide, was not even shortlisted in the post-Brexit process of relocating the European Medicines Agency and the European Banking Authority from London should give politicians some food for thought.

Bridge building is particularly necessary to meet the challenges of migration from third countries. With additional back-up measures in place, Vienna could encourage new paths of cooperation such as incentivizing increased voluntary admissions of refugees in neighbouring countries and promoting city/town partnerships and exchanges of best practices on a community- and city-level where integration actually happens. Improving mutual understanding between Eastern and Western EU member states is crucial. However, current opposition to France and Germany regarding the EU's medium term financial framework, law suits against nuclear power plants in the East, and the proposal to cut family allowances for children of Austrian workers living outside of Austria might prove to be counter-productive. The focus should rather be on issues that really account for major budgetary losses, such as unfair tax competition, tax evasion, and tax avoidance.

Questions related to the labour market are traditionally very important in Austria, but they are often dealt with in a rather isolated way. Yet, more than anything else, its performance is linked to the overall economic and political situation. Therefore, all decisions related to reforming the European Union should be taken against the background of jobs and growth.

Austria should continue to stress the importance of the Western Balkan states path towards EU membership, but could also use it as a lever to speed up the reform process of the Union. A reformed EU must be up and running when the next batch of countries join the Union, otherwise there will be no enlargement at all.

To strengthen its political weight in Europe, consensus needs to be built first and foremost within Austria based on a mutual understanding of all major political and civil actors. Joint positions will be key in the debate on the future of Europe. At the end of the day, building a better Union is about the added value of being European. Much more than a country's size, it is its priorities, creative ideas, and strategic partnerships that really matter.

Belgium in Search of a Stance on Today's EU Integration Dilemmas

Nathalie Brack and Amandine Crespy

Despite the multiple crises Europe currently faces, the salience of EU affairs in Belgium remains low and popular support for the EU above average. However, since the main party in the governing coalition, the Nieuw-Vlaamse Alliantie (N-VA), decided to exit the long-standing Belgian pro-EU consensus by labelling itself Eurorealist, Belgium's voice in EU affairs seems to be fading. The latent tensions between the governing parties lead to a crucial lack of ambition and impact on the debates on Brexit and on the future of European integration.

A Political Pivot away from Federalism Against the Background of the EU's Low Salience

The EU tends to be a "non-issue" in Belgian politics. Despite the economic crisis and Brexit, the salience of European matters has remained low and the Europeanization of political parties is rather limited. The "permissive consensus" still seems firmly embedded in Belgium as

N. Brack (✉) • A. Crespy
Institut d'Etudes Européennes, CEVIPOL, Brussels, Belgium
e-mail: nathalie.brack@ulb.ac.be; acrespy@ulb.ac.be

M. Kaeding et al. (eds.), *The Future of Europe*,
https://doi.org/10.1007/978-3-319-93046-6_2

Euroscepticism has little support. According to the latest Eurobarometer survey, 62% of Belgian citizens consider EU membership as a good thing, 61% are optimistic about the future of the EU, and 53% trust the EU (well above the EU28 average). Citizens who are Eurosceptic are still a small minority which tend to turn to radical (left or right) parties to express their dissatisfaction with EU policies as no other party is willing to articulate their discontent.

Indeed, it is not surprising, given the low level of salience among the public, that EU issues are not politicized among Belgian political parties. Across all parties, there has historically been a pro-integration consensus.

However, this pro-European consensus has been recently challenged by the N-VA, which received the majority of votes in Flanders and Belgium in the 2014 regional and federal elections. The N-VA sensibly shifted its stance to a (self-proclaimed) "Eurorealist" position. The party calls for reforms of the EU and its policies, but it does not question the integration process or the EU as such. The party asks for a reflexion on the division of powers between the EU and the member states (or the regions) but is not opposed to further integration, especially in the policy areas relating to the market and security (currency, defence, migration, internal market, energy).

Typically, the N-VA calls for a "stronger Flanders in a stronger Europe", a slogan that does not conceal the party's contradictions when it comes to territorial secession. Flemish nationalists have endorsed a number of the critiques expressed by Brexiters, claiming that this should be a "wake up" call for the EU to engage with reforms that strengthen its border and security policies. However, internal tensions have appeared as some radical nationalists have taken the opportunity to call for a Flemish exit from Belgium, a position that is not a part of the party's establishment, which has favoured a strategy of slowly hollowing out the Belgian Federal State. The N-VA has furthermore profiled itself as a trouble maker in the EU political order by proactively organising the exile of the Catalan independentist leader, Carles Puigdemont, in Brussels.

On the other side of the political spectrum (and linguistic border), grass-root contestation is sporadically triggered by specific European issues at the national level, such as the CETA and TAFTA/TTIP debates. Since the Francophone Socialist Party (PS) is in the opposition at the federal level, it tends to take a more critical standpoint on specific EU-policies such as trade and the economy. Paul Magnette (Minister President of Wallonia at the time of Brexit) labelled himself the "first Social Democratic Eurosceptic".

A Lack of Ambition or a Balancing Act of the Governing Coalition

Because of these new developments, it seems that Belgium's voice in Europe is fading.

Belgium has long been a custodian of the integration process. But such pro-activity seems to have disappeared, as the current government seems rather passive in the Brexit debates as well as on the future of Europe. Of course, there is a growing consensus that frank discussions about both the nature and the limits of European integration are becoming unavoidable in the current context of crisis. But there does not seem to be any agreement on Belgium's position in these discussions. This is mainly due to two elements. First, more and more member states have adopted a transactional approach to European integration, which has led to Belgium's isolation in its defence of an "ever closer union". Second, and more importantly, the divergent positions of the two main parties of the governing coalition (the Francophone Liberals [MR] and the Flemish nationalists [NVA]) make it difficult to have a strong, clear-cut position on Europe. At first, the Prime Minister was quite proactive and defended the option of a multi-speed Europe. It was one of the key points of the Benelux vision on the future of Europe. But if we look closer, there is not much substance behind the broad idea of a "multi-speed Europe". The MR (to which both the Prime Minister and Minister for Foreign Affairs belong) still defends the longstanding Belgian position regarding European integration, while the multi-speed Europe scenario is supposed to deepen the integration process in a context of increasing diversity among member states. The N-VA, on the other hand, pleads for more flexibility within the EU: no European "supergovernment imposing choices to Member States and regions" but a flexible EU with several circles of Member States depending on the public policy concerned. It should go beyond a "two-speed Europe," as the party is against the idea of a "core EU" that sets the tone for the others. In addition to that, the two regions will be impacted differently by Brexit: Flanders is very dependent on the UK for its import/export and focuses on the economic aspects of future cooperation, which is also evidenced in the N-VA discourse on the future of Europe. In Wallonia, in contrast, the pleas for a more social and more democratic Europe are enduring.

These tensions between defending the regional/national interest on the one hand and the long-standing EU position on the other lead to a passive atmosphere within the Belgian government regarding the EU. Each position it takes seems like a balancing act between contradictory positions. As a result, Belgium's voice seems somewhat absent from current EU affairs.

In conclusion, it is high time for the country's main parties to acknowledge publicly that the historically inherited federalist consensus, whereby EU policies and the goal of an ever-closer union were unquestioned, is now over. Subsequently, there is an urgent need for better concertation in order for Belgium to be able to shape the future of the EU, for instance in the coming French-German discussions about differentiated integration and the future of the euro area.

Bulgaria: More Europe in Domestic Politics

Daniel Smilov

If the EU disintegrates or withdraws into a smaller western European core, Bulgaria and the Balkans will become a contested region between Turkey, Russia, and possibly even China. This will lead to instability and potential conflicts. Democracy in the Balkan countries would hardly survive, but it most probably would degenerate further into some form of semi- or open authoritarianism.

Luckily this is not the most probable scenario, but it cannot be excluded from reckoning. The governments of Bulgaria and Romania demonstrate that they are conscious of this scenario, and partly because of that these are two of the most pro-European member states. The population at large holds a similar attitude towards the EU, although there has been some significant erosion of trust in the Union since 2007. Currently, roughly half of the Bulgarians trust the EU.

The weakness of Balkan democracies cannot be attributed solely to their communist past and the lack of an entrenched democratic political culture. Eastern Europe has become a laboratory of political trends that are common throughout the whole of Europe. These include the rise of populism and nationalistic conservatism, which has been responsible for

D. Smilov (✉)
Centre for Liberal Strategies, Sofia, Bulgaria
e-mail: daniel@cls-sofia.org

M. Kaeding et al. (eds.), *The Future of Europe*,
https://doi.org/10.1007/978-3-319-93046-6_3

events like Brexit. Because democratic institutions in Eastern Europe have relatively shallow roots, these trends have swept through the region much more profoundly than in Western countries. Poland and Hungary are today's flag bearers of national populism, which is socially very conservative and generally sceptical of enhanced European integration.

Bulgaria is affected by this political trend as well, but Bulgaria is different from the mentioned Visegrád duo in at least three important ways. First, Bulgaria has an external border of the EU and is also Turkey's neighbour. Bulgarians know that in the case of a serious influx of refugees, they will need European solidarity to cope with it.

Second, unlike Poland and Hungary, Bulgaria is not ethnically or religiously homogeneous: the Turkish minority is around 10% of the population, and around that share of the population is Muslim. So, despite official discourse, Bulgaria is *de facto* multi-cultural.

Finally, due to its proportional electoral system, Bulgarian politics is run by complex and difficult coalitions. A single party has not enjoyed a parliamentary majority for decades in the country, which has led to messy and frustrating coalition bargaining. But this has also prevented one party to become dominant in the public sphere as in the cases of Poland and Hungary.

On the negative side, the weakness of complex coalition governments has made them much more susceptible to strong economic interests. This explains Bulgaria's perennial problems of corruption (at the high end of government), of the lack of an independent judiciary, and of a disappearing free media.

The EU has been instrumental in helping Bulgaria deal with the state capture problem. Monitoring within the Cooperation and Verification Mechanism (CVM) run by the EU Commission has identified problems and pressed the Bulgarian government to introduce meaningful reforms. But over recent years, European pressure has diminished as the EU has been preoccupied with the euro crisis, Brexit, and more pressing problems present in Hungary and Poland.

In January 2018, Bulgaria started its first term as a rotating president of the EU Council. The CVM was not lifted, which is a clear demonstration that the domestic tasks on corruption and judicial reform set by the Mechanism has not been done. Yet, the Bulgarian government has outlined a very pro-European agenda and has set sensible priorities like integrating western Balkan states into the EU.

The Bulgarian case primarily demonstrates that the success of the EU depends on its capacity to penetrate member states' domestic politics. The pre-accession period was one of the most successful in Bulgarian history because joining the EU was a strong motivating force for reforms. If the Union fails to serve such a function, it could become just a contingently instrumental tool for national elites who want to shift the blame on the supranational institution for potential failures.

How could the EU be more influential in domestic politics? Of course, steps towards federalising external border protection, creating a genuine European defence institution, and strengthening the eurozone will be helpful. Bulgaria has made membership in the eurozone its top priority, so it will be a constructive player in regards to further integration proposals. Because radical institutional reforms towards federalisation are unlikely to happen in the near future, one possible path of development is to strengthen the main pan-European parties' role: the conservatives (EPP), the socialists (PES), and the liberals (ALDE). They could contribute to the development of a common European public sphere by regularly taking positions on domestic issues in the member states, by discussing national electoral platforms, and by showing solidarity with their sister parties much more energetically. Whenever needed, they should criticise their partners effectively and put pressure on them to change course.

The Bulgarian Socialist Party, for instance, is a member of PES and its former leader, Sergei Stanishev, is even the current president of this organisation. Despite this, his own party has taken some strongly pro-Russian positions in domestic politics. Recently, the party has become a fierce critic of the Istanbul Convention on preventing and combating violence against women because of the inclusion of the word "gender" in it. Such anti-European positions have become the focus of intense domestic debate, but the point is that they should be meaningfully discussed at the European level as well.

Part of the problem of the EU is that under a pro-European gloss, domestic politics in many states has taken a decidedly anti-European turn. This becomes a focus of European attention only when a major problem happens like Brexit or the Greek crisis in the eurozone. But such reactions are already too late. Therefore, the European dimension of domestic politics should be increased if the EU is to be a stable polity.

One positive sign is the fact that over the last several years, elections in France, Germany, the Netherlands, and Austria have become a truly pan-European affair. Eastern Europe should be monitored by the European public exactly in the same way because often Eastern Europe portrays a picture of the future for the continent as a whole.

Croatia: Finally in the EU but Still in Search for a Place Under the (EU) Sun

Jakša Puljiz

Accession to the European Union has been a long-standing goal of Croatia's foreign policy ever since it proclaimed independence from the former Yugoslavia in 1991. This goal had finally been achieved in July 2013, much later than initially expected. Croatia has passed the longest and the most demanding accession negotiations of all new member states from Central and Eastern Europe, and one would expect that it is rather prepared to compete in the single market. However, as the economic crisis of 2008 has revealed, Croatia still faces many structural difficulties that have made its economic recovery the longest among member states, with the exception of Greece. Positive economic trends in the last couple of years were insufficient to counter the effects of prolonged economic crisis and increased job opportunities in Germany, Ireland, and other member states with much higher wages. Consequently, the long-standing problem of a diminishing domestic demographic situation has been further exacerbated after the accession, as emigration has reached record levels in the last two years. In short, Croatia's European dream that was nominally fulfilled by the accession to the EU is still far from materialisation in the sense of

J. Puljiz (✉)
Institute for Development and International Relations, Zagreb, Croatia
e-mail: jpuljiz@irmo.hr

M. Kaeding et al. (eds.), *The Future of Europe*,
https://doi.org/10.1007/978-3-319-93046-6_4

achieving lasting clear economic and social benefits. On the contrary, Croatia's position has slipped from one of the most developed transition economies in 1990 to the bottom of the Central and Eastern European economies. While the bloody dissolution of the former Yugoslavia should be acknowledged as a great contributing factor to such an outcome, the sustained deficiencies in the Croatian economic governance system and other related factors are still slowing down its economic recovery and have kept the country from catching up with the rest of the EU.

The current Croatian government continues its work to complete the European integration process by finalizing the preparations for entering the Schengen area. In addition, the government has clearly stated, for the first time, its goal of entering the euro area by 2022. It has published a strategy for the adoption of the euro together with the Croatian National Bank. These two processes are marked as top political priorities with regards to Croatia's position in the EU. However, entering the Schengen area is under question due to the unresolved border dispute with Slovenia. In 2015, Croatia retreated from the arbitration process after a scandal broke out related to a misdemeanour of one of the arbiters on the Slovenian side. However, the arbitration court continued its work and proclaimed its decision on the land and maritime border. With the divergent positions on the result of the arbitration decision in mind, the impact of the border dispute on entering the Schengen area should not been underestimated. With regard to the latter goal, some political and social actors expressed their scepticism and fear that the Croatian economy will not be adequately prepared for the adoption of the euro by that time.

Other relevant EU-related priorities include supporting the enlargement process of other countries in South-Eastern Europe and securing the external border of the EU, with special reference to migrants and refugees entering the EU via the so-called Balkan route. Croatia is vitally interested in its neighbouring countries admittance into the EU as this would imply stability throughout the whole region, and moreover, it would improve economic prospects. But the process of accession is far from being easy and straightforward, especially in the case of Bosnia and Herzegovina. Furthermore, unresolved bilateral issues from the 1990s such as border definitions with Serbia and Montenegro or issues of missing persons from the Homeland War could easily raise tensions between the countries and slow down the accession process.

In the case of migration and refugee flows, lessons learned from the dramatic events in 2015 should help Croatia as well as other EU member states on the Balkan route to enhance mutual cooperation in managing the flows through a common approach. All the countries on the route are determined to avoid a situation similar to the one experienced in 2015, but the real test of whether they are indeed ready for such a coordinated approach has not yet occurred.

Regarding the debate on the future of the EU, Croatia is not in favour of further differentiation in the level of integration between member states. Strengthening of a "multi-speed Europe" is seen as a threat to the non-core countries, as they could become real outsiders within the EU. In that respect, Croatia is taking and will continue to take a more pro-EU stance in comparison to some other Central and Eastern European countries, which has already been visible in matters like the discussion on migration policy. Croatia will look to promote a more inclusive approach in future integration processes. For example, it will try to shape the process of bringing balanced benefits to all member states so that everybody gets a chance to participate in the continuing integration process. How exactly this could be achieved remains an open question not just for Croatia, but for all actors involved in the debate.

To conclude, Croatia's primary political goal remains the finalization of the European integration process, i.e. joining the Schengen area and eurozone. Fulfilment of these two goals would bring Croatia closer to the core group of member states if such a group would be established in the future. A more integrated Croatia would also be a significant gain for the future enlargement process of other South-Eastern European countries to the EU, and a final political and economic stabilization of this part of Europe.

A Future Europe for Cyprus: A Struggle to Overcome the Utopianism of the 1990s and Come to Terms with the Tough Pragmatism of the 2020s

Giorgos Kentas

Ever since the debate on the future of the EU was launched on 1 March 2017, not much discussion was discerned in Cyprus. There were some occasional opportunities for citizens to contemplate on the future of the Union, such as a Citizens' Dialogue on the European Commission's *White Paper* that was held in Nicosia in May 2017 in the presence of the Commission Vice-President J. Katainen and held by the European Commission Representation. Very few articles appeared in local newspapers while even fewer TV or radio talk shows tackled the issue. It is also very hard to detect any substantial discussion on social media on the subject matter.

This should not come as a surprise. The EU hardly makes the headlines in Cyprus, and when it does, it is for the wrong reasons. Across the island, there is a prevalent view that suggests that a small country like Cyprus cannot make any difference on the course of the EU. This, however, is an

G. Kentas (✉)
Department of Politics and Governance, University of Nicosia, Nicosia, Cyprus
e-mail: kentas.g@unic.ac.cy

M. Kaeding et al. (eds.), *The Future of Europe*,
https://doi.org/10.1007/978-3-319-93046-6_5

epiphenomenon of a deeply traumatized public. Although Cypriots feel proud of their participation in the Union and the eurozone, they concurrently believe that the EU failed them over two crucial issues. First, the EU made very little contribution to fostering the re-unification of the island and its emancipation of the malign role of historic guarantor powers. Second, EU institutions are blamed for the notorious bail-in arrangement in 2013 that triggered the worst financial, employment, and income crisis on the island since the Turkish invasion in 1974.

It is odd to observe how sharply Cypriots shifted from being unconditional Euroenthusiasts to becoming qualified Eurosceptics within only a couple of years as shown by Eurobarometer surveys. Their eagerness to join the Union seems to have proved much more idealistic than the tough pragmatism of the Union's day-to-day business. The first European Parliament Elections in Cyprus (held in 2004) marked a historically low voter turnout of 72.50%, but compared to the all-time low as seen in the latest European Parliament Elections that came close to 44% (43.97%), that could have even been considered an ideal participation percentage. Cypriots however still maintain a strong normative view about the image the EU needs to have, an image of solidarity. They believe in a Union that must be able to offer economic and financial stability, job security, physical security, and political security.

A strong normative image of the EU as a resilient and effective security community always stands out in public debates and is often instrumentalised by political elites in an effort to get the attention of an increasingly more sceptic public. This effort, which illustrates both a deep divide between elites and the public and a potential bridging point for communicating the interest of the country to stay ever closer to the project of European integration, emanates from two major fronts. One concerns the economic image and the potential of the country. EU membership, elites argue, is the country's strongest asset, a point of attraction, and a card of trust for non-EU countries. According to this view, companies and entrepreneurs find Cyprus a secure, trustworthy place to do business and invest their money. After the 2013 crash, however, a good part of the public appears very sceptical, agnostic at best, of whether the country's economic situation would have been better off if Cyprus did not join the eurozone in 2008. It is true that public perceptions are not always amenable to subjective lines of argumentation.

The other major front that illustrates the normative image of the EU as a security community relates to the territorial problem of the island: the division between the areas under the effective control of the Government of the Republic of Cyprus and the areas under the effective, yet illegitimate, control of the Turkish army. The two communities of Cyprus, the Greek Cypriots and the Turkish Cypriots, have struggled for more than 54 years to bring the political affairs in Cyprus under normality. EU membership is considered a sufficient condition for augmenting the sense of security on the island. There is no agreement as to how this could be substantiated and materialized in the framework of a comprehensive settlement between both these divided communities and between other major stakeholders. The EU is willing to help, but it has some limits that must be better understood.

In the context of the debate about the future of the EU, it may be high time for Cypriots, both the elites and the public, to reflect on more pragmatic grounds. A good starting point is to begin wondering not on how much the Union can offer to them, but how much they can offer to make the Union stronger, more effective, and more efficient in tackling the challenges that concern them the most. All five scenarios of the Commission's *White Paper* could be suitable, but the one that allows willing Member States to do more together in specific areas seems to be most appropriate.

Like many other EU Member States, Cyprus is primed to be engaged in some tough and challenging regional developments in the next ten, 30, and probably 50 years. Cyprus' political identity is profoundly anchored in the Union, but its geopolitical and geoeconomic destiny is embedded in the Eastern Mediterranean and the Middle East. The discovery of considerable natural gas reserves in Cyprus' (and neighbouring countries') territorial waters and the potential to discover even bigger reserves (or even oil) has revealed a new era in the region. As a result, a number of bilateral, trilateral, and multilateral arrangements and projects ensued that touch upon core issues that concern the forces shaping the future of the EU.

All these developments open a great opportunity to be seized by other EU member states that are already involved in the region, such as Greece, Italy, and France, who can work together with Cyprus in fostering a regional community of interest that will involve other non-EU member states, such as Israel, Egypt, Lebanon, Jordan, and the Palestinian Authority. That community will build upon EU and national resources to constitute an invaluable asset to the Union in dealing with urgent issues, such as regional security, energy security, environmental security, migrant crises, organized crime, illicit trafficking of weapons and other hazardous material, and finally terrorism.

On that account, a future Europe should include institutions, resources, and mechanisms that can allow member states to seize regional opportunities to build upon their joint resources in order to add tangible value to the Union and its citizens, as well as to extend the normative power of the EU to other regions. By all means, such an arrangement would certainly be beneficial to Cyprus and its people.

Czech Republic: A Paradise for Eurosceptics?

Petr Kratochvíl and Zdeněk Sychra

The Czech Republic is a peculiar case of a persistently Eurosceptic country. Despite the fact that the country´s economy has been growing very fast in recent years and its unemployment rate is the lowest in the EU, recent Eurobarometer opinion polls suggest that Czechs express more wariness regarding European integration than the notoriously Eurosceptic Brits. Czech Euroscepticism consists of a mixture of the dashed hopes of a fast catching up process with the richer EU member states, the traditional Czech suspicion towards great powers, and a pinch of the general Czech dislike of grand visions of any kind.

Against this general background, it has been easy for Czech policymakers and media to frame the recent crises (such as the eurozone crisis and the more visible migration crisis) as the failures of the EU. In particular, issues related to migration have grown to gargantuan proportions in the public's imagination. The highly politicized migrant distribution mechanism has gained a central position in the minds of many Czechs as

P. Kratochvíl (✉)
Institute of International Relations, Prague, Czech Republic
e-mail: kratochvil@iir.cz

Z. Sychra
Faculty of Social Studies, Masaryk University, Brno, Czech Republic
e-mail: sychra@apps.fss.muni.cz

M. Kaeding et al. (eds.), *The Future of Europe*,
https://doi.org/10.1007/978-3-319-93046-6_6

an example of why the country should not engage in deeper integration into the EU's core.

The consequences of this are twofold. First, Euroscepticism and outright EU-bashing has become acceptable even in the political mainstream. Expressions of a positive attitude towards the EU are seen at best as signs of political naiveté and at worst as a betrayal of the country's real interests.

Second, it is increasingly difficult to distinguish between the left and right Eurosceptics, who were originally starkly opposed to each other. Those on the left rejected the EU as a neoliberal project aimed at the quasi-colonial exploitation of poorer member states, while some on the right saw the EU as overly socialist and bureaucratic. Today, these two wings are increasingly united around a re-emerging nationalist agenda, advocating the return to the mysterious "traditional" values.

However, the Czech political leadership is still hardly comparable to strongly ideological regional figures such as Kaczyński and Orbán. To the contrary, the new Prime Minister, billionaire Andrej Babiš, is a purely pragmatic leader who is not interested in foreign policy at all. European integration becomes relevant only when it affects his international reputation, his domestic preferences, or his business.

What to Do? Traditional Answers

In this vagueness lies the seed of the potential Czech contribution to the integration process. Unlike the governments in Poland and Hungary, which seek a conservative revolution, one Czech government after another shy away from grand gestures that would radically change the country's foreign policy trajectory. Many long-term priorities therefore remain firmly in place, and it is highly unlikely that they are going to change in the foreseeable future. These priorities include (1) the Eastern Partnership, (2) the Western Balkans, and (3) the economic openness of the EU.

The Eastern Partnership is in deep crisis pertaining first to the partner countries themselves and second to the accompanying EU policy as the EU's priorities lie elsewhere at the moment. As a relaunch of the project is badly needed, the Czech Republic can tap both its traditional ties to these countries as well as its experience with the EU Presidency and the related launch of the Eastern Partnership in Prague in 2009.

The EU enlargement to the Western Balkans is also deeply problematic, albeit for a different set of reasons. However, the Western Balkans are one of the areas where the Visegrád Four have not yet lost their clout. The concerted activities of the Four, including the financial support of the International Visegrád Fund, could bring about some progress.

Finally, Czech policy-makers are well aware of the country's dependence on external factors, as exports constitute more than 80% of the Czech GDP. Any Czech government will thus vigorously support the EU's trade openness. While this topic is not much discussed in the public, any threat to this openness would undoubtedly call forth substantive actions of the government in favour of a continuous flow of free trade.

What to Do? Novel Approaches

Simultaneously, new priorities emerge which are related to the actions required by the public or which can respond to the worries citizens feel. A referendum on Czexit is not a chimera on the horizon, but something the current Czech discussions about introducing the general referendum brings even closer. At the same time, many of the Czech citizens' worries can be effectively addressed only with concerted efforts on a broader regional scale, most conveniently in the EU framework. Three such issues that can swing the public opinion both ways have gained more prominence recently – the worries about East-West double standards, fair taxation/the fight against tax evasion, and the protection of EU external borders.

Take, for instance, the sensitive issue of double standards of food products. If the issue is presented more generally as the necessity for a better functioning internal market (which it, in the end, really is), Czech initiatives here can both contribute to overcoming real East-West divisions and simultaneously improve the Single Market's operation. A similar reasoning, which connects domestic concerns with the broader functioning of the EU, can be applied to tax evasion as this was one of the main campaign topics for the current Prime Minister. The new government will be more than willing to show that its domestic anti-fraud struggle is supported by an EU-wide strategy, which the government is an active part of. The third issue is the protection of the EU's external borders. The Czech political elites, in their efforts to show that they are in favour of solidarity with other EU member states, will be prepared not only for diplomatic activities on this front, but also for a financial contribution which would back diplomatic efforts.

Czechs are not born as Eurosceptics – their negative views of the EU are largely the result of the political disconnect between domestic concerns and broader EU-related issues. If this fundamental problem is overcome, the Czech Republic has the potential to become an active member state again with a clearly defined agenda, which will be appreciated both by the Czech public and by the country´s partners abroad.

The Schizophrenic Danes

Marlene Wind

Everybody seems to love Denmark. Or do they? Well, if one managed to take a stroll in the center of Paris at Christmas time last year, the traditional stylish shopping mall Le BHV just across the old town hall celebrated a true Noel Danois. The French may have a special crush on Denmark as the country is going through a period of intense 'Denmark-hype' led by the dynamic young President Macron. He loves Danish TV-series, flexicurity, our social-liberal model – and not least the Danish Commissioner Margrethe Vestager who he sees as an obvious candidate to lead the next European Commission.

The love is, however, not quite requited – though probably welcomed by our competent Danish Commissioner. And even though it's always nice to get attention, the sudden French courting is probably less appreciated by the current Danish center-right government which is struggling to find its feet in a new post-Brexit Europe.

Fortunately, and as opposed to what many predicted, Brexit does not seem to undermine the European project. In fact, it may intensify it. Everyone can see what a kamikaze-mission the UK is on at the moment and what exiting the EU actually means, which certainly "helps". However, an

M. Wind (✉)
Centre for European Politics, University of Copenhagen,
Copenhagen, Denmark
e-mail: mwi@ifs.ku.dk

M. Kaeding et al. (eds.), *The Future of Europe*,
https://doi.org/10.1007/978-3-319-93046-6_7

intensified, energized, and fast-moving EU is almost a nightmare for Denmark, as we fear being left in the cold with our three remaining opt-outs. The Danes have recently tried to garner new friends and allies after Brexit and have even gone so far as to visit Victor Orbán in Budapest in a (perhaps) misunderstood desperate attempt to look for new allies. Holland is a more obvious new friend. However, it is important to remember that while the Dutch may have come to look more like the Danes in recent years by wanting less rather than more Europe, they are still firmly situated at the heart of Europe: part of the eurozone and without opt-outs.

Danish Troubled Waters

What not only the current Danish government but the entire Danish establishment is increasingly realizing (but only vocal about behind closed doors) is the fact that we – no matter how we twist and turn it – will be further isolated if or rather when the EU gains new momentum. Denmark has always – like the Brits who joined the EU at the same time we did – been pragmatic about Europe. We were mainly in it for the money. Unlike the Brits, however, the Danes always knew that they needed to preserve access to the Single Market. Danish civil servants have spent most of their time over the past 20 years attempting to circumvent the Danish exemptions in all kinds of ways. So, while there is little risk the Danes will follow the Brits out of the door as opinion polls show strong support for staying in the EU, the Danish government is gradually realizing that the EU will not be the same after Brexit. What are the options then for a small self-marginalized member state in a Europe where Macron – in order to get the European project back on track – speaks of a Europe in different speeds with the euro at its core? There is certainly something to be worried about: PESCO, Banking Union, and closer coordination among the eurozone countries do put Denmark under strain. We have to remember however that it was the Danes themselves who invented the idea of a multi-speed Europe by voting no to the Maastricht Treaty in 1992 and insisting on *permanent* opt-outs to the euro, defense, justice, home affairs and EU-citizenship. The deal was that we could stay in Europe at a lower level of integration but not prevent the rest from moving on together. Until now, the reluctant Brits have been able to prevent this from happening. However, as the slowest ship in the convoy is no longer there, there will be no way in which Denmark can prevent the European supertanker from setting ashore in the future by conquering new territory.

Whether the current (or future) government likes it or not, Denmark clearly should try to stay as closely connected as possible to the European core and try not to drift into the periphery. Maybe Denmark doesn't belong among the vanguards and feels more comfortable among the laggards, but staying as close to the core as possible means that we may at least be heard when others shape our European future. And Denmark has traditionally been good at influencing the European agenda despite our opt-outs. It would of course be much better to get entirely rid of the exemptions (the European citizenship opt-out is already today irrelevant as the Amsterdam Treaty secured that European citizenship should not replace national citizenship). However, three opt-outs remain, and shifting Danish governments have already tried to rid themselves of two of them in referendums. In 2000, the Danes rejected the euro (again), and in 2015, we said no to amending our opt-out in the justice-and home affairs area to an opt-in solution (similar to the one the Brits have). Very few politicians including the current government have an appetite for trying again. As there were 15 years between the two previous referenda, one can only imagine when another government may dare to consult the Danes again. The best a Danish government can do is thus to stay relevant and be as close to the Eurozone as possible. Joining the Banking Union would be a good first step, and the current government is in fact considering exactly that. Not least because it can be realized without a referendum, joining is not entirely unrealistic. In 2019, a committee will come up with its recommendation. Considering that Denmark has one of the EU's largest financial sectors (measured per capita), several things suggest that it may in fact be favorable.

However, apart from trying to stay relevant and working hard within the EU institutions and frameworks, Danish politicians should also start sharing their visions about Europe to the public. Politicians always complain when they lose a referendum that the Danes have not understood the importance of the European project. However, why are they surprised when politicians stay silent on the EU as soon as a referendum or an EP election is off the table? If we do hear of Europe, it is mostly about how it has failed. The refugee crisis in 2015 is a good example, as Danish politicians (probably like politicians in many other countries) were immensely busy blaming Europe for its failure and incompetence. And this is despite the fact that those who really were to blame were the member states themselves.

Politicians should also start to discuss sovereignty. Both in Denmark and in the UK, polls show that this is an issue that really concerns people. Sovereignty is, however, wrongly regarded as something you either fully possess or may lose entirely: a zero-sum game. This logic is very much opposed to the thinking proposed by Macron in his Sorbonne speech last year where he repeatedly spoke of sovereignty as something that you only *gain* by being part of Europe. You become more – not less – powerful, important, and able to act in the world when you join forces with other countries. Indeed, the Brits may soon enough discover that they will lose rather than gain sovereignty from being outside the European club. They will become the new 'rule takers' rather than rule makers. The same can happen to Denmark if we end up in Europe's periphery after Brexit. And this cannot be easily remedied – not even by a beautiful Danish Christmas in Paris and Margrethe Vestager.

Has the Estonian e-Tiger Been Caught Napping?

Viljar Veebel

Modern digital technologies have fundamentally reshaped the ways of how our society functions today. We are able to communicate over large distances at an unprecedented speed, share our views with thousands of people at the same time, analyse big data sets, and easily manage large administrative systems.

The gains of digital technologies are well known in Estonia. Already in 1997, Estonia introduced e-Governance to provide public services online. E-taxation, internet voting, e-health solutions, the e-Residency project, and other digital solutions followed. Today, about 99.5% of public services provided by the state are available as e-services. E-solutions constitute a significant part of Estonia's identity and the country is considered a trail-blazer in the international arena. Justifiably, the magazine "Wired" called Estonia "the most advanced digital society in the world", and Estonians are extremely keen on maintaining this progressive image.

Most recently, the European Union has also put a particular emphasis on matters related to e-solutions. In early 2017, the European Parliament published the report, "On e-democracy in the European Union: Potential

V. Veebel (✉)
Estonian Foreign Policy Institute, Tallinn, Estonia

M. Kaeding et al. (eds.), *The Future of Europe*,
https://doi.org/10.1007/978-3-319-93046-6_8

and Challenges", which focuses on ways to improve traditional democratic systems by digital means. It discusses the so-called e-Democracy tools that combine various ICT technologies to increase people's participation at the EU decision-making level. However, what looks relatively easy on paper could be extremely difficult to implement in practice. Estonia, as a digital pioneer, has faced many challenges, and not everything has gone smoothly. Thus, the country has valuable experience in introducing digital services which could be useful for the EU to develop a new, digitally-advanced union.

Estonia's experience in implementing digital solutions allows us to highlight two issues. First, they can only operate properly if people trust the state, the community, and the system as a whole. Second, enhanced extensive coordination is needed in terms of planning, resource pooling, and allocation.

The authorities involved in developing digital services in Estonia have emphasised that the public's confidence in digital solutions is determined by both the actual technical functioning of the systems and the way people perceive how digital solutions are functioning. The biggest technical "failure" of Estonia's digital systems occurred in autumn 2017 when a security risk was discovered in the certificates of Estonians' ID-cards, which operate as a personalized key to digital services. Whereas the probable culprit is the producer of the chips, the problem stirred up the public and caused relative embarrassment and harm to the responsible authorities. Even if it is obvious that complex systems will periodically go through problems, this experience has seriously damaged the reputation of Estonia as a digital pioneer and reminded the country that the more large-scale and complex the digital systems are (should we, for example, talk about systems covering the whole population of the EU), the higher the risk of technical failures is. This does not have to mean a super database; it could simply be a hardware component vital for the whole system. Thus, the first lesson for the EU is that only properly functioning technical solutions resistant to overloading, cyber-attacks, and other digital threats can contribute to the transparency of democratic processes in the EU and bring Europe closer to its citizens. Simultaneously, there is another threat apart from technical errors. Even if no significant technical errors occur in real terms, people could still feel that digital solutions are not working in a transparent way. Thus, a second lesson for the EU should be that in addition to minimizing technical errors when introducing digital solutions, it is important to build public confidence in digital solutions and show that they are safe and credible. In this regard, the EU in particular, which is facing internal tensions between the EU member states and the EU institutions, should think more strategically when introducing new extensive digital solutions. It should be combined with strategic communication that is focused on increasing people's sense of ownership over digital solutions.

Last but not least, extensive and enhanced coordination is needed when planning and budgeting digital solutions. Estonia's experience in introducing digital health solutions (which include a system of digital receipts, digital registration, and digital medical data with digital medical images) has been rather negative in the early years of the project. The main problems identified later on were associated with too much "paper" coverage of the projects, excessive focus on only one subtopic in practice (i.e. on the system of digital receipts), lack of general coordination, and unnecessary duplication of both activities and resources. Similar problems could easily occur at the European level when developing trans-European digital networks. This again raises delicate issues of both coordination mechanisms and division of responsibilities and power at the European level. It will definitely be an interesting time when the ideas about EU-wide digital solutions will be in much clearer focus.

Altogether, keeping all these potential downsides in mind, there is a lot to be gained from increasing accessibility to different and hitherto heavily "bureaucratic" services at the EU level. Two priorities could be named in this respect. First, the EU should try to open up its legislative process, especially the one formerly known by the name of comitology. Even if the effects are visible only in the longer term, there is much to gain from it. Second, one should share and reuse data that is already collected, because collecting the same data multiple times is very expensive. This issue is already comprehensively investigated by a pan-European consortium that, under the leadership of the Tallinn University of Technology, attempts to pilot the so-called *once-only principle* in the EU and beyond. The project aims to reduce the administrative burden on businesses and public administrations. As the European Commission sees it, the project ensures that information is supplied to public administrations only once regardless of the company's country of origin.

To conclude, Estonia has an impressive past as the e-Tiger, offering revolutionary solutions both for local society as well as best practices for the whole EU. However, the recent crises and lack of new inventions in the last years indicate clearly that the e-Tiger requires a sound wake-up call, as it currently runs the risk of falling into deep dreams about is digital superiority instead of having decisive efforts towards achieving new success stories.

Bridging the EU's Political Dividing Lines Is in Finland's Security Interest

Juha Jokela

The years of several severe European crises have shifted the debate and policy on the EU in Finland into a more reserved and hesitant direction. Finland joined the EU in 1995 largely due to economic and security reasons. It wholeheartedly embraced the opportunities of European integration, and it built a distinctly pro-EU profile in comparison to its closest reference countries, the other Nordic states. Iceland and Norway have decided to stay outside the EU, yet they are members of the European Economic Area. Among its Nordic EU peers, Finns have gained the reputation of being the most pro-integrationist in comparison to the opt-out obsessed Danes who joined the EU in 1973 and self-reliant Swedes who joined in 1995. Finland is the only Nordic EU member which has adopted the euro.

There has been some political discussion concerning Finland's influence, as well as its constructive approach towards EU decision-making throughout its membership. Yet it was the eurozone crisis that re-politicized EU affairs in Finland. The rescue loan packages turned out to

J. Jokela (✉)
Finnish Institute of International Affairs, Helsinki, Finland
e-mail: juha.jokela@fiia.fi

M. Kaeding et al. (eds.), *The Future of Europe*,
https://doi.org/10.1007/978-3-319-93046-6_9

be politically toxic for consecutive Finnish governments. They also contributed to the rapid emergence of the openly populist and Eurosceptic Finns Party, which altered the political landscape of the country. The public support for the party, however, dramatically decreased after it entered into a coalition government in 2015, and the party has recently split. Moreover, the worsened European security environment has again highlighted the role of the EU for Finnish security, not least because the country is not a member of NATO.

Despite political turbulence linked to the European crises, the public support for the EU and the euro has remained high throughout the last years. The most recent Eurobarometer (Autumn 2017) suggests that 53% of the Finns trust in the EU, 57% are optimistic of its future, and 75% are for the euro. The exposed negative implications of Brexit for the UK, the recent return to the economic growth in Finland, and the victories of pro-European forces in France and elsewhere have clearly increased optimism towards the European Union in Finland. At the same time, new challenges and threats, including authoritarian tendencies in parts of Europe, terrorism, and a more competitive and unstable international environment, are acknowledged as notable challenges for the Union.

Recommendations

Finland has highlighted the unity of, and solidarity in, the EU as a response to the rapidly worsened European security environment, and most notably to Russia's more assertive foreign policy and its proven willingness to resort to military power. The heightened tensions have also resulted in increased military activity and security concerns in the Baltic Sea region. This largely explains why Finland has emphasised the EU's unity in its response to the Ukraine crisis and the Russian annexation of Crimea. Moreover, Finland has been one of the top supporters of recent efforts to deepen the EU's defence cooperation, and it has underlined the importance of the EU's mutual assistance and solidarity clauses in the field of security and defence.

Helsinki should, however, bear in mind that unity and solidarity in one of the key fields of European integration is concomitant to the solidarity and unity in the other fields. Hence it should be in Finland's interests to bridge the political divide between north and south within the euro area as well as the east and west over migration pressures. This requires a constructive approach and willingness to seek compromises rather than to set rigid national red lines in EU decision-making.

Concerning the stability of the single currency, Finland has rightly underlined national responsibility over public finances, the importance of market discipline, and the ability to strike national economic reforms and improve competitiveness. Yet the economic rationale to pool resources in order to address asymmetric macroeconomic shocks as well as risks in the banking sector should be more openly discussed as these were key features of Finland's own past economic crises. In terms of the euro area governance, proposals resisting the setup of parallel structures and safeguarding the integrity of the EU's institutional and legal frameworks are clearly in the interests of smaller members.

Finland should also adopt a constructive approach towards the negotiations concerning the new multi-annual financial framework marked with negative implications of Brexit on EU spending. Many of the country's EU priorities require adequate funding. These include securing external borders and managing migration, support for innovation and research, and deeper defence cooperation. Finland is right to highlight the efficacy of EU spending, including thorough assessments of the added value of EU level spending.

While the migration crises and entry of more than 32.000 asylum seekers largely through Sweden in 2015 resulted in notable political polarization in Finland, the difficulties at its eastern border with Russia underlined that Finland could also be an entry point of significant irregular migration to the EU. Around 1.800 asylum seekers suddenly entered the country from Russia during the winter of 2015-16. Securing the EU's external borders, addressing the root causes of migration pressure through effective EU foreign policy, moving towards a common asylum policy, and creating a permanent relocation system should be a priority for Finland.

Finally, given the relatively high support for the EU, reflected in opinion polls and continued electoral success of the pro-EU political parties, the political polarization in EU affairs seems to be a lesser problem in Finland than it is often assumed. The perception of polarization is largely upheld by a relatively small yet loud political minority, as their populist arguments often make headlines. Yet the EU has surely, and rightly so, become an increasingly political question in Finland. Therefore, political actors should engage in a debate on EU policies and concrete EU reform proposals.

Much of the recent national EU discussion has focused on Finland's influence in EU decision-making amid the changing political dynamics of the EU. This is, of course, important for a relatively small member state, yet the politicization of EU affairs suggests that the electorate is at least equally interested in the substance of EU policies. That is what the political parties aim to achieve in terms of EU policies and reforms with much desired influence in the EU. More focus on policy objectives would help the electorate ponder where the differences of the parties' EU agendas lie.

France: Supporting the Jobless – A Job for Europe

Xavier Ragot and Olivier Rozenberg

The election of Emmanuel Macron as President of France in May 2017 was clearly a defence of the EU project in front of sceptical opponents. There are now high expectations that France will have the ability to propose and lead new European initiatives.

Macron's view to circumvent political disagreement in the EU is to accept that various groups of countries can progress at differing speeds. This would allow some core countries (including France and Germany) to integrate further on some key issues before convincing other member states to join. Consistent with this view, he pushed forward some proposals that may concern either a group of countries (on taxation or a common defence policy), the eurozone (creating the position of a finance minister, a budget, and parliament) or Europe as a whole (on a European intelligence academy or a European asylum agency).

X. Ragot
Department of Economics and OFCE, Sciences Po, Paris, France
e-mail: xavier.ragot@sciencespo.fr

O. Rozenberg (✉)
Centre for European Studies and Comparative Politics, Sciences Po, Paris, France
e-mail: olivier.rozenberg@sciencespo.fr

M. Kaeding et al. (eds.), *The Future of Europe*,
https://doi.org/10.1007/978-3-319-93046-6_10

One should obviously acknowledge the political clarity of the message, its legitimate voluntarist approach, and the political realism of some propositions. Indeed, there seems to be a kind of momentum around Macron's vision for Europe. After developing his thoughts in a speech in La Sorbonne in September 2017, he has been announced as the recipient for the 2018 Charlemagne Price.

However, we see two kinds of limits to his project, which lead us to develop an alternative proposal.

The first one is domestic and political. French voters are in the middle of rankings on support for European integration, but their positions are, as elsewhere, strongly correlated to social status. The working class divorced from Brussels years ago. More distinctively than in many other member states, successful populist forces are focussing their discourse on opposing the EU. It is essential therefore that major moves during the integration process address the concerns of popular classes. Macron understood it as indicated by his efforts on the Posted Workers directive. Yet, it is unclear whether his European dream speaks, as a whole, to the poor and the blue-collar workers.

The second doubt is more geopolitical. Macron's key proposal – a budget for the eurozone – raises opposition from other member states, especially Germany. Its additional cost can be perceived negatively. Also, the focus put on an instrument (a budget) rather than on a policy end weakens the proposal. And the risk is high that, in the end, a typical Brussels compromise would end in pretending to create a new budget without proper commitment.

More generally, it seems to us that a proposal for European reforms must fulfil three requirements: it must be politically feasible, it must improve the popular ownership of the European project, and finally it must improve economic and social efficiency in Europe. The European re-assurance scheme we are proposing satisfies these conditions.

The European employment insurance scheme is an old idea. It dates back at least to the Marjolin report in 1975 and the McDougall 1997 report. This old idea was rejuvenated after the crisis. Proposals for such a move have been made by the French treasury in 2014 and the Council of Economic Advisors in 2015, as well as by the Italian government in 2015. Various German institutions, covering a large spectrum of the political debate, now study it. The diversity of studies and interest is a sign of political feasibility, or at least of political interest.

The reason behind it is the strong economic and social argument in favour of such a scheme. One of the most debated propositions is a re-insurance scheme mimicking the US system (but adapted to the European situation). The idea is to keep the heterogeneity of the unemployment scheme at the national level and to introduce an additional layer of European insurance, which is activated during deep recessions in any European country to extend the duration of unemployment benefits. The European level could finance additional months of high-level benefits or contribute to the financing of long-term unemployed for countries with very high duration, such as Belgium.

Such a scheme would first keep the heterogeneity of unemployment systems within Europe by adapting to the heterogeneity of labour market institutions and may also be the result of national preferences that must obviously be respected.

This being said, there is scope to increase risk sharing across European countries during recessions. Indeed, the cost of macroeconomic stabilization relies too much on fragile workers going through long periods of unemployment. The traditional moral hazard argument, which limits the amount of insurance provided to the unemployed to keep incentives right, is not convincing during those periods, where these fragile workers have a hard time to find a job.

The financing of the extra-layer of insurance would require some member states to contribute in order to ensure that the system is balanced over the medium-run. The US system, for example, is based on some *clawbacks* and *experience ratings* conditions, which are devices to determine fair contributions over the medium run. The key property is that the evolution of the contributions is made after the recession during the recovery period.

Such a scheme would provide an automatic stabilizer at the European level. The Commission (at least) now recognizes the need to have a countercyclical economic device to sustain aggregate demand in the eurozone in various contributions. A European unemployment scheme is a powerful tool, as we know from national experience, because the propensity for unemployed workers to use additional resources for consummation is high. The ability to finance this European layer by debt issuance during recession would maximize the stabilizing properties of the scheme, although it is not necessary for the scheme to exist. Indeed, the very idea of eurobonds is still hard to discuss in some countries.

Apart from this proposal, and coherently with it, Macron's idea to align the basics of welfare, labor law, and tax systems between France and

Germany appear to be particularly promising, albeit difficult to implement. The progressive reduction of the gaps in those fields will send the signal that European integration can be deepened to avoid greater dumping between member states. As for trade agreements, there is also an advantage to move first on convergence: France and Germany could settle policy norms on those three key policy fields before others join. Aligning basic norms on labor, taxes, and welfare could indeed be the next frontier for the European continent.

Germany and the EU: Managing Differentiation to Avoid Structural Segregation

Andreas Maurer

Germany's European policy is conditioned by three challenges. First, the negotiations on the next Multiannual Financial Framework (MFF) contextualise Berlin's considerations on how to tackle a post-Brexit budget with growing demands for more European spending. Given that Germany will hold the Presidency of the Council of the European Union in the second half of 2020, the government must combine its priorities with its role to broker the end-game. Second, the European Parliament elections in May 2019 display the uncomfortable context of any "big reform" debate on the EU. Brexit forces countries to compensate for London's share of contributions to the EU's resources. Combine Brexit with the uncertainty surrounding the future alliances of the Italian 5Star Movement and Macron's "en marche" and you realise the major dynamics in the various political groups. In any event, Berlin's ability of yesteryear to project its grand coalition into a similar alliance within the EU-Parliament is more than uncertain when the Parliament is likely to mutate into an imponder-

A. Maurer (✉)
Department of Political Science, University of Innsbruck, Innsbruck, Austria
e-mail: Andreas.Maurer@uibk.ac.at

M. Kaeding et al. (eds.), *The Future of Europe*,
https://doi.org/10.1007/978-3-319-93046-6_11

able, if not erratic, actor that risks blocking major reform initiatives. Against this backdrop, ideas to escape this unknown future by combining differentiated integration with the means of intergovernmental procedures and institutions may flourish. Macron's related proposals for a eurozone budget, a European Finance Minister, and the safeguarding of such core's decisions by national parliaments represent a traditional French strategy to bypass supranational actors such as the Commission, the Court of Justice, and the Parliament and to decide within the core by unanimity. While Merkel might continue to support ideas for such a differentiated, intergovernmental Europe, the SPD and others are likely to block attempts that risk structural segregation and a de facto dismantling of the EU's supranational strength. Third, the bullying Trump administration's trade-war policy displays Germany's economic weakness. Export giants are vulnerable to protectionist action by third countries. If Trump follows up on his repeated threats to slap tariffs on imports, the EU will realise that Germany is the weakest link in protecting the EU's economy on a global scale.

Investing in the Social Market Economy

In a nutshell, Germany's EU policy is to focus on four challenges. First, economic and social imbalances are putting cohesion and solidarity within the EU to the test. For a country that is heavily dependent on an economically healthy environment, government politicians underline that the country cannot content itself with the fact it is doing well right now. They rightly argue to invest not only at home, but also in Europe. Two projects are connected with these reflections: the process towards the adoption of the next MFF and the further deepening of the Economic and Monetary Union (EMU). Berlin shares the Commission's analysis that the EU is called to do more and that it will have to spend more, even after Brexit. To the surprise of many EU politicians, the grand coalition agreement of 2018 not only stresses that budgetary discipline remains crucial, but also that Germany is willing to pay more into the EU budget! In addition, the coalition supports specific funding of economic stabilization, social convergence, and structural reform in the eurozone. As expected, the government intends to strengthen and reform the eurozone in close partnership with France to make the currency more resistant to global crises. The European Stability Mechanism (ESM) should be reformed into a European Monetary Fund under parliamentary control and permanently anchored within EU law. Of course, the government also signals some key conditions for realizing its commitment: the EU should push for fair taxation and avoid a race to the bottom. The introduction of a financial transaction tax is likely to be linked to the MFF debates. At first glance, Berlin's announcement to pay more into the EU budget seems to represent a U-turn in the country's traditional stance for less spending and better fiscal discipline. But a closer look reveals that additional payments are not the result of altruism and unconditional solidarity. Contrary to widespread public and published opinion, Germany is most likely the largest net beneficiary of the EU's internal market. According to this analysis, a distorted narrative of Europe has long been deeply engrained in the day-to-day political consciousness in Germany. Investing into EU cohesion funds has been defined as a burden on the Germans. The recent announcement to contribute more should thus be understood as the government's confession that the traditional "net-payer" argument is dishonest.

Fixing Breaking Points on the EU's Founding Principles

Second, the refugee and migration crisis causes a deep rift, particularly between Berlin and other member states that hold Germany responsible for the migration flows to Europe. Neither Germany nor Greece or Italy can solve the migration challenge alone. Berlin will therefore continue to promote joint management of migration, and a fair distribution of incoming migrants among all EU members. Rogue moves like Orban's endeavour to prevent any "foreign populations" from settling in the country inevitably clash with EU law. The refugee-relocation crisis thus leads to a third key challenge for Germany's EU policy: how should the EU react to the idea marked as "illiberal democracy"? To keep the EU based on the rule of law and democracy, the Merkel administration calls for defending this foundation on the domestic – and European – fronts to remain a credible partner on the international scene. Linking the MFF debate with the migration and rule of law disputes, Merkel considered connecting EU subsidy pay-outs to structurally weak regions with refugee relocation on several occasions. Moreover, a majority of the German Bundestag would support the idea to make the payment of EU funding dependent on the respect of rule of law principles.

Strengthening the EU's Collective Voice and Arranging for Instruments

Fourth, Germany supports a further deepening towards a genuine European foreign and security policy to defend EU interests. The EU's internal rifts create a target for seeds of deep division sown from the outside. In this regard, Berlin does not only refer to the isolationist-aggressive Trump administration or Russia's attempts to unsettle its neighbouring countries in Europe's east, but also to China's investment policy that is driving a wedge into the EU with its "16 (CEEC) + 1 (China)" initiative.

Overcoming Internal Constraints

Many German politicians have voiced their support for more EU-integration, despite obviously having different viewpoints on specific topics. Most senior politicians still strive for an ever closer union. However, proposals such as those made by Macron are unlikely to be answered quickly. While Merkel and the SPD might be convinced that the EU requires a major overhaul, others are more sceptical and wary of any steps that could bolster the extreme right AfD. The key challenge for the German government is to end misguided home-made narratives and to stand firm on the EU's – added – values: (1) Germany is a net-contributor but above all an economic net-beneficiary of European integration, (2) migration cannot be mitigated by isolating Mediterranean countries, and (3) differentiation must be settled within the EU's political and legal framework.

Greece: Of "Future of Europe" Plans and Political Honesty

Xenophon Yataganas and A. D. Papagiannidis

The debate over "The Future of Europe" is of preeminent – not to say of existential – importance for Greece if the country is to resume its progress after too many years in deep financial, economic, and increasingly social crisis.

High-visibility events that cause equally high expectations, such as Emmanuel Macron's visionary Europe address at the Pnyx, with the Acropolis as its backdrop, have raised the stakes in Greece, especially considering the difficulties arising from an upswing of Euro-hesitant (to say the least) sentiment in Greek public opinion over "Europe" that have replaced long-standing, resolute Euro-phile positions.

Still, the fundamentals of keeping the country anchored to the European edifice throughout this period of reassessment and rebuilding "Europe" remain constant. Four main political reasons come to mind. First, Greece

X. Yataganas (✉)
Greek Center of European Studies and Research, European Public Law Organisation, Athens, Greece
e-mail: xyatagan@otenet.gr

A. D. Papagiannidis
European Public Law Organisation, Athens, Greece

M. Kaeding et al. (eds.), *The Future of Europe*,
https://doi.org/10.1007/978-3-319-93046-6_12

is a small country in the ever-troubled neighborhood of the Eastern Mediterranean and the Balkans. Second, nationalism and irredentism are alive and well. Third, the refugee/migrant issue continues to simmer in the country. Finally, Greece is in a situation of shifting alliances and of an international fluctuation in the balance of power.

Economic reasons may be less evident but they nonetheless remain important. Just compare Greece of the late seventies to today's country, even after 7 years of deep crisis and the loss of some 25% of its GDP. The amount of infrastructure built, of agricultural production support, and of the integration of goods-and-services in Europe-centered value chains makes any thought of sliding off a changing Europe deeply disturbing. Even in the bitter period of austerity, the support of European partners has not only been forthcoming to save the day in fiscal terms, but also to salvage the banking system.

The setback in EU popularity in Greece – as is the case in many other European countries – has one main cause: the economic crisis, with the halt in growth and in incomes in many countries that is erroneously attributed by public opinion to the EU (a perception, which is often reinforced by national governments). True enough, the upswing in growth taking place nowadays in most of the EU puts a brake to the Euro-hesitant slide of opinion, alongside the realization that the Brexit adventure and the flirtation of countries like France or the Netherlands with extremist/anti-European "solutions" are cost-inducing.

In Greece, though, the trend we are discussing has been compounded by the severity of the austerity packages with which the eurozone rescue operation was inextricably associated. In what appears to be an unavoidable political reflex ex post facto, successive governments were prompt to attribute the pain incurred by the proverbial man in-the-street to "Europe". Add this to the widely-shared tendency in the Greek public debate to take some sort of moral high ground by advocating an EU with better democratic and social credentials. In such an approach, the Union should seek a closer convergence between stronger and weaker member states. Also, the emergence of a "German Europe" is feared.

It is in this overall context that the main wagers placed within a "Future of Europe" framework are faced. To take just a few examples out of the current reform proposals:

- A common defense policy – or even a gradual build-up towards such a policy – could well have positive effects for the security environment in Greece (being one of the few EU countries with military expenditure meeting or even surpassing the NATO-mandated share of 2% of GDP). The same goes for a common foreign policy. Still, one should not avoid the crucial question on both counts: to what extent would potential EU-derived priorities e.g. in deployment of forces, or even more importantly in the Cyprus issue or the future of EU/FYRoM relations, correspond to what are considered the minima of Greek national interests? If the "Future of Europe" discussion is to really address fundamental issues, it will have to recognize areas where essential sensitivities are in play and look for inclusive answers.

- Giving effectiveness to FRONTEX and evolving towards a credible EU Border and Coastguard Agency would also be important from a Greek point of view, provided it does not end up in causing a Nauru effect. The design of an EU position in this matter should focus more on the reality of those European countries (Greece and Italy) that bear the brunt of the refugee/migrant wave.
- Shifting to the package of proposals affecting the future of the eurozone and of the Economic and Monetary Union: the recent adventure Greece has lived through would seem to militate in favour of shifting the ESM towards a European Monetary Fund, seeking a common Finance Minister, and/or establishing a eurozone budget with federal undertones. Here again, the underlying question should in no way be avoided: would such steps of a federal nature be compatible with a country with a fundamentally weaker fiscal situation? Or, looking at the current negotiations to deepen the Banking Union: how far could the mutualisation of debt (especially of legacy debt) be discussed under the current German political equilibrium? Also in this case, those participating in discussions on the "Future of Europe" have to accept the fact that if principles that exclude countries with weaker fundamentals are adhered to, the end-result will be less "Europe".

What does this brief overview add up to? The realization that Greece, like most small EU countries, should approach the idea of a multiple-speed integration (under whatever name) with circumspection.

In the current outlook of European affairs, apart from offering itself as a test case of how far the "weaker link" situation does not preclude integration, Greece can also contribute to the discussion because of its geopolitical situation. Efforts to stabilize the Western Balkans play partly on the diplomatic work currently underway to find a solution to the Greece/FYRoM issue. Also the tenuous equilibrium of EU – Turkey relations depends to quite an extent on the capability (and willingness) of the Aegean islands to endure the strain of the refugee/migrant presence.

Last, but by no means least, the temptation to reach a "Future of Europe" consensus through a de facto "Directoire" approach, however virtuous the federal intentions are said to be, should be resisted. Political honesty should be the name of the game throughout these discussions. In that respect, the role of Greece can be perceived as a constant reminder of the extent to which efforts are needed to keep the discussion up and running.

Hungary: Becoming Pioneers Again

Péter Balázs

Hungary and Poland were the two countries that started the tremendous transformation process in Central and Eastern Europe by the late 1980s. Their names have been commemorated in the well-known acronym of the PHARE programme (Poland-Hungary Aid to Economic Reconstruction).

Throughout the EU accession talks, the Hungarian negotiators and their Polish colleagues preserved their pioneering role in taking initiatives and finding novel solutions to emerging problems. However, at the 2010 parliamentary elections, the nationalist-conservative Fidesz party returned to power and immediately launched a permanent political campaign filled with high anti-western emotions and aided by constructed conflicts. The first new "enemy" of Hungary was the IMF. Shortly after followed an aggressive and durable campaign against "Brussels", which symbolised the power centre and the institutions of the European Union (however, not including NATO residing in the same capital). After his re-election in 2014, Prime Minister Victor Orbán eliminated the last defenders of the "Euro-Atlantic" attachment in Hungary from the Ministry of Foreign Affairs and transformed this institution into the "Ministry of Foreign

P. Balázs (✉)
Center for European Neighborhood Studies, Central European University,
Budapest, Hungary
e-mail: balazsp@ceu.edu

M. Kaeding et al. (eds.), *The Future of Europe*,
https://doi.org/10.1007/978-3-319-93046-6_13

Trade and External Relations" that focuses mainly on the non-European area. Hungary performed a total U-turn by re-orientating the country from the western world of values, norms, rules, and institutions towards eastern models of high power concentration.

The EU was taken by surprise when Viktor Orbán declared in 2011 that his favourite state structure is not the liberal, but the "illiberal" democracy. This construction is, by definition, nonsense, as remarked by Angela Merkel at her Budapest press conference held with Orbán in February 2015. In fact, the "illiberal" adjective could hardly comply with the concept of "democracy". In Orbán's perception, "illiberal" means a high degree of power concentration that limit the impact of democratic checks and balances (both rules and institutions) and neglect human rights' norms.

Acting against the EU from the inside is relatively easy. As the whole integration system is based on voluntary cooperation between the member states, enforcement measures were not believed necessary from the outset. Deviations from the rules have been handled mainly in the framework of two procedures: excessive deficit and infringement.

The only legal device to discipline unruly member states is Article 7 TEU foreseeing the suspension of certain rights of the member state. This provision, which has never been applied before, was invoked against Poland in 2017. However, some difficulties occur in connection with the use of Article 7. The "serious breach of the EU's values" has to be determined in the Council by unanimity, but any accused member state would find at least one friend to use its veto at this point, as the example of the mutual support between Poland and Hungary proves.

The confrontational behaviour of some new member states in front of the EU's corrective action is a new phenomenon as well. In this perception, nationalist-populist movements depict the EU as an external adversary trimming the field of action of sovereign and independent states. This attitude expresses the negation of existing legal and moral obligations and contests the balance between rights and obligations.

With the above background, it is extremely strenuous to recommend concrete measures. The most frequently proposed sanctions are to stop the transfer of EU funds, to suspend voting rights, or to temporarily exclude the member state from Council activities. However, any of these measures would not instigate the resisting member state to remedy the problem; on the contrary, the government in question would see an additional opportunity to elevate the conflict with the EU further and present the whole case to its domestic public as another justification for the initial breach of EU norms. The Polish and Hungarian governments' reactions in 2017 presented abundant examples to underpin this thesis. Confrontational behaviour in those member states also traps the political opposition. If the opposition takes the EU's side and supports, for example, the suspension of the transfer of EU funds as a just reaction, it is immediately declared by the governing majority as "unpatriotic, the enemy of the nation and homeland, etc."

The emergence of anti-integrationist extreme right political forces in Europe marks the end of the general "permissive consensus" granting almost unlimited support to the smooth functioning and the further expansion of EU integration. If extremists are in the government like in Poland or Hungary, they become direct players in the EU Council and may threaten the unity and equilibrium of the whole system. At this point, the main question is the general attitude of the EU community. As long as the gap exists between hardliner defenders of EU norms calling for sanctions and tolerant supporters of those breaching the common rules, no progress can be expected. On January 5, 2018, Viktor Orbán was the special guest of the German CSU at its "Klausurtagung" in Seeon, Bavaria. His home press reported this event as a great diplomatic success proving the recognition of his xenophobic refugee politics. How could any EU retaliation measure counterbalance that political effect?

Hungary – together with Poland – was at the forefront of systemic transformation and among the first to join NATO and the EU. The attachment to European norms and values has deep historical roots in both countries. There are abundant political and intellectual capacities for large contributions to common solutions of new problems for European integration under changing conditions in the world. However, those forces have been excluded from governments, and their positions are threatened and weakened in opposition, too.

The EU should take clear and firm positions on the application of its own norms and values. Ambiguous, friendly-looking politeness with norm-breakers does not solve problems but destroys the already decreasing credibility of the EU inside and outside the organisation. The EU should also closely survey coming elections in new member states because this is the only way that leads to changes.

Active Participation, an Icelandic-German Alliance and United Nordic Front

Baldur Thorhallsson

Iceland is closely associated with the European Union through its membership in the European Economic Area (EEA) and the Schengen Agreement, as well as other cooperation agreements. The structure of the EEA Agreement makes it difficult for the EFTA (European Free Trade Association)/EEA states to shape the future direction of the EU and the EEA. Their future direction is inherently intertwined due to the hegemonic role of the EU and its member states vis-a-vis the EFTA/EEA states within the EEA framework.

The current coalition government, which took office in Iceland on 30 November 2017, firmly opposes membership to the EU. However, the government's platform does not mention the possibility to formally withdraw Iceland's EU membership application submitted in 2009, which was put on hold in 2013. Iceland's accession process began nine months after the country's economic crash in October 2008. In early 2015, the government stated that it no longer regarded Iceland as a candidate country to join the EU but did not withdraw its EU membership application.

B. Thorhallsson (✉)
Institute of International Affairs and Faculty of Political Science,
University of Iceland, Reykjavik, Iceland
e-mail: baldurt@hi.is

M. Kaeding et al. (eds.), *The Future of Europe*,
https://doi.org/10.1007/978-3-319-93046-6_14

Accordingly, Iceland is not in the groups of the EU's candidate countries, but the EU has stated that Iceland would be welcomed to resume the accession process at any stage and it has never stated that Iceland is not a candidate country.

In any case, the government is firmly committed to the EEA Agreement. In fact, it regards the management of the Agreement as one of Iceland's most important foreign policy objectives. Importantly, there is a cross-party consensus about the EEA Agreement, and politicians rarely criticise the country's Schengen membership.

Despite this commitment, Iceland has not been able to have a say on the future direction of the EU and the EEA. Therefore, Iceland has to find a new strategy in order to influence the future of the EU/EEA.

Concrete Recommendations

We propose a new threefold strategy for Iceland.

First, Iceland should set up a special team of European experts within the Ministry of Foreign Affairs, which would be responsible for scrutinizing proposals from EU member states and EU institutions on the future of the EU, if such proposals may have any bearing on the EEA Agreement. The team could draw upon the expertise in other ministries and governmental institutions in order to evaluate the pros and cons of the proposals in Iceland's interests. Accordingly, Iceland would identify key areas or issues of interest (such as the role of the European Commission, the Brexit negotiations, free movement of people, and enlargement), prioritize them, and present a policy response to the EU, EFTA member states, and EU institutions. Iceland would become active in the debate on the future of Europe and attempt to have a critical voice on the future structure of the EU and the EEA. The team could work in a similar manner as the Brexit team within the Icelandic government.

Second, Iceland should make Germany its main ally in Europe. Iceland and Germany were close during the post-war period, and there are considerable German interests in Icelandic political and cultural affairs, which was noticeable during the Icelandic accession process to join the EU. Iceland should take advantage of this interest and further utilize its new political niche, its newly discovered Arctic identity, and its strategic location in the High North (both in regards to the Arctic sea road's opening and Russia's increased military activity in the Arctic and the North Atlantic) in order to make German decision-makers more willing to form a formal alliance on security, defence, and economic matters concerning the EEA, Schengen, and NATO. For instance, the proposed alliance could include regular high-level consultation meetings between both politicians and officials of the two states before EU and NATO summits and meetings of the EEA Council and the Arctic Council. Furthermore, Icelandic ministers and politicians could prioritize meetings with their German counterparts, political parties could strengthen their ties with their sister parties in Germany, and the Icelandic Foreign Service could increase its activity in Berlin by assisting Icelandic companies and other relevant actors, such as research and cultural institutions, to establish closer ties with Germany. This new Icelandic strategy would be consistent with the present Norwegian strategy to make Germany its main ally in Europe.

Third, Iceland should establish closer bilateral and multilateral relations with Nordic states on European Affairs. Iceland could advocate for a common Nordic response to proposals on the future of Europe. A common Nordic position would not only strengthen the position of Iceland and Norway in shaping the future of the EU, but it would also strengthen the position of the Nordic member states of the EU within the Union's framework. The Nordic Council would be an ideal place for consultation and coordination of Nordic responses to proposals on the future of Europe. Moreover, the three Baltic states, which work with the Nordic Council, could be brought into this Nordic (-Baltic) cooperation framework on the future of Europe. The three Nordic EU member states have a seat at the negotiation table on the future of Europe within the decision-making structure of the EU and are more likely than other member states to understand and take up Icelandic interests in such a forum. Furthermore, should Iceland and Norway create a common response to proposals on the future of the EU, it would strengthen both states in their attempt to have a say on the future of Europe. While the Nordic states are already working closer on specific EU policies such as the EU energy policy within the Nordic Council, the proposed cooperation would take the current relationship a step further.

To summarize, Icelandic governments have failed to engage in the European debate on the future direction of the EU and the EEA. A new active strategy is needed in order for Icelandic political (including security and defence) and economic interests to be taken into account in discussions on Europe's future. A new threefold strategy which would consist of making changes to policy-making at home and active engagement abroad, an Iceland-German alliance, and a united Nordic front could improve Iceland's performance on the future direction of the EU and the EEA.

Ireland and the EU: A Pragmatic Approach to Integration

Cian McCarthy

State of Play

Public support for EU membership in Ireland is amongst the highest of any member state, and it has been steadily growing. In a recent poll, it was found that 88% of Irish people think that the country should remain a member of the EU. The same poll showed that 87% of people believed that Ireland has benefited from its membership in the EU. That these two numbers are almost identical is neither coincidental nor surprising. Although it would be unfair to characterise the Irish approach to the EU as transactional, it would be equally mistaken to say that Irish support for the EU is based purely on ideology and values. Ireland has traditionally taken a pragmatic approach to the EU and the integration process.

Another explanation of the recent increase in support of Ireland's membership is a reaction to the British decision to withdraw from the EU and the uncertainty that has followed, which have galvanised Irish support for the Union. The willingness of the European Union to prioritise the concerns of Ireland, and the commitment not to move ahead in negotiations

C. McCarthy (✉)
Institute of International and European Affairs, Dublin, Ireland
e-mail: cian.mccarthy@iiea.com

M. Kaeding et al. (eds.), *The Future of Europe*,
https://doi.org/10.1007/978-3-319-93046-6_15

without Irish consent, have also demonstrated that Ireland is stronger as a member state than it would be alone.

This is emblematic of Ireland's pivot towards Europe and away from the UK since its EU accession in 1973. Before accession, Ireland was politically and economically shackled to the UK with two-thirds of exports going to Britain and the Irish punt fixed to the pound sterling. Today, exports to Britain account for closer to 15% of Irish exports, and Ireland is a member of the Economic and Monetary Union. While for many in Britain the EU has diminished the UK's sovereignty, for Ireland it has enhanced sovereignty by amplifying its voice on the global stage and emancipating the country from the UK. Brexit will only push Ireland closer towards the EU and has already spurred the Irish government to seek new policy allies and trading relationships from within the EU.

The Irish government has taken the task of reorienting Ireland within an EU of 27 Member States seriously. It has engaged with organisations such as the Institute of International and European Affairs and European Movement, in response to the European Commission's call to foster a citizen-centric debate on the Future of the EU.

Takeaways

Irish European policy strikes a balance between proactive European engagement and the preservation of distinctive national interests. In most cases, the Irish national interest is aligned with EU integration. There are some areas, however, in which tensions exist between the two.

The combination of Brexit and the election of President Trump has reignited the discussion about EU defence cooperation. The former provides the opportunity for a revived Franco-German engine to pursue further integration, and the latter presents an incentive for European leaders who no longer trust that the EU can solely rely on the US and NATO for protection. Any involvement of Ireland in a common European defence would require not only an adjustment in long-standing government policy, but also a referendum to change the Constitution. The Irish Defence Forces, however, have taken an active role in peacekeeping and humanitarian operations, such as rescue operations in the Mediterranean, and have also participated in the EU framework with participation in the NATO partnership for Peace and PESCO to achieve high levels of interoperability.

Crucial questions for Ireland arise from the current debate on the future of European defence. To what level can Ireland engage with initiatives of the Common Security and Defence Policy without, for instance, undermining the state's policies and commitment to peace-keeping and non-proliferation? How can Ireland reconcile military neutrality with its commitment to political solidarity with other EU member states? And crucially, will Ireland's reluctance to join a common defence affect our position at the core of the EU? These questions need to be addressed in Ireland.

The first step towards answering these questions could be the formulation of a National Security Strategy by the Irish Government. The most recent statements of Irish Foreign Policy were published before the UK's decision to leave the EU, and therefore a recalibration is necessary. This strategy would outline how Ireland, both at a national and European level, can provide for the security of its citizens and in doing so would improve public understanding of the new threats facing the country, such as cyber-security and hybrid threats, and of the benefit that international cooperation can provide in tackling these threats.

Another potential policy divergence between Ireland and EU institutions is over proposed moves towards further harmonisation of corporate tax policies. For Ireland, tax competition is not seen to belie solidarity. Instead, it is considered to be a valuable mechanism for small and geographically peripheral states to counterbalance the comparative advantages that some other member states hold, due to economies of scale and proximity to larger markets.

Having said that, Ireland can still play a role in tackling excessive tax avoidance by multinational corporations and individuals. The Irish position, however, is that these actions, along with any other international tax regime, are best managed at the global level through the OECD rather than at a regional level by the EU.

Finally, there are many areas in which Ireland is proactively supporting greater integration and cooperation at the European level. The government has joined the "Digital 9", a group of digital frontrunners who aim to achieve the completion of the Digital Single Market; Ireland supports reforms that will deepen the Economic and Monetary Union, such as the completion of the Banking Union, Capital Markets Union, and the introduction of the European Deposit Insurance Scheme, that should mitigate potential future crises; and there is much support in Ireland for the expansion of the EU budget – funded by new internal resources – that is put towards projects that embody European added-value. Ireland is committed to being a core member of the European Union and to supporting new avenues of integration and cooperation, but as has been true in the past, public support for new forms of cooperation will only be secured if the people and the government see the benefits of such integration as outweighing any negative effects on Ireland's distinctive national interests.

Italy and the EU: A Relationship with Uncertain Outcomes

Sergio Fabbrini

From Love to Dissatisfaction

Italy has moved from being one of the most pro-European countries to one of the most Eurosceptic. The 1992 Maastricht Treaty opened a new era in Italy-EU relations. The Treaty introduced new, radical macroeconomic criteria for entering the newly instituted Economic and Monetary Union (EMU) that asked for a substantial overhaul of the Italian budgetary process. The Italian negotiators of the Treaty accepted them on the assumption that Italy needed an "external constraint" for introducing domestic reforms. Their strategy worked successfully but it was also costly. Indeed, after the sacrifices of the late 1990s, the 2000s were a decade of postponed reforms of both economic and administrative structures. When the financial crisis exploded in 2008-2009, its consequences struck a powerful blow to the unreformed Italian system. The following decade constituted the most dramatic period in the economic life of the country, as the financial crisis' harsh social repercussions were

S. Fabbrini (✉)
School of Government, Libera Università Internazionale degli Studi Sociali, Roma, Italy
e-mail: sfabbrini@luiss.it

M. Kaeding et al. (eds.), *The Future of Europe*,
https://doi.org/10.1007/978-3-319-93046-6_16

comparable only to wartimes. Constrained by EMU decisions and approved intergovernmental treaties, Italy had to introduce reforms that not only, after long last, called into question vested corporate interests, but also generated dramatic social problems. Not surprisingly, a Eurobarometer survey released in August 2017 reported that a total of 86% of Italians considered their economic situation as "rather" or "very" bad (compared to an average of 51% in the EU28), or only 36% of Italians said that they trust the EU (compared to an average of 42% in the EU28). The same Eurobarometer recorded that, for the Italians, unemployment and immigration constituted the most pressing issues the country faces, issues where the role of the EU was either complicit or marginal. Finally, the elections of March 4, 2018 showed the dramatic impact of those issues on the political behaviour of the voters. The elections led to the spectacular success of the 5Stars Movement in the south, which proposed a guaranteed basic income for the unemployed, and of the League in the north, which called for the expulsion of 600,000 illegal immigrants.

From Dissatisfaction to Reaction

During the previous Italian parliamentary mandate (2013–2018), the three governments, which were supported by basically the same parliamentary majority, inevitably became entangled in strained relationships with the EMU institutions and, in particular, with those member states that were more engaged in preserving the economic logic of austerity that prolonged the Italian crisis. The Italian governments reacted more and more openly to the ordo-liberal orthodoxy and insisted on an interpretation of the Stability and Growth Pact, which considered the economic conditions of each member state. For the Italian governments, growth had to take the same status as stability; the pro-cyclical effects of domestic reforms had to be balanced by the counter-cyclical approach of EMU policies. Italy was finally able to introduce some flexibility into its budgetary policy, but the rationale of the Pact did not change. The governments needed flexibility because the logic of "external constraint" was no longer accepted by significant sectors of the population. New political entrepreneurs, such as the 5Star Movement, the League, and the radical left, capitalized on the unrest generated by the financial and migratory crises and accused the EU of being the culprit of all of Italy's difficulties. The March 4, 2018 elections, indeed, showed that these parties received the support of more than 50% of voters.

The Elections: 'Ital-exit' or Reform

The parliamentary elections were the functional equivalent of the referendum in the United Kingdom that led to Brexit in June 2016. The winners were two anti-EU parties. The League, emerging as the main party of the centre-right coalition, and the 5Stars Movement, which identifies itself as a post-ideological party. Both are populist and nationalist parties, although for different reasons. They both ran on anti-EU platforms and accused the EU of being an organization controlled by technocrats and serving multinational and cosmopolitan interests. The 5Stars Movement retained its promise to organize a referendum on Italy's participation in the eurozone, although it was not a central issue of its campaign. The League focused on the need to take back control of Italy's borders in order to keep immigrants out of the country. Both parties refused de facto to consider the Maastricht's criteria as indisputable and proposed to increase public debt through a guaranteed basic income or public deficit through a radical tax reduction. This approach was supported by more than half of the voters. The elections show that Italy's attitude towards the EU more closely aligns with the Visegrád group's, which aims to empty the EU from within rather than to secede from it, which the British chose to do.

The losers of the elections (the centre-left Democratic Party [PD] and the moderate centre-right Go Italy) ran pro-EU campaigns. Of particular note, the PD supported a view that might be considered congenial with the strategy of differentiated integration. Their main proposals asked for improving the EMU fiscal framework in order to boost structural reforms and investments, for advancing towards a European fiscal stance, for controlling macro-economic imbalances as well as deficit spending, for transforming the European Stability Mechanism into a European Monetary Fund, for creating a European finance minister operating within the Commission, and, finally and above all, for completing the Banking Union through the introduction of its third pillar, the European Deposit Insurance Scheme. The PD also proposed to strengthen the Juncker plan by focusing on innovation-driven investments through a coordinated corporate taxation policy. The party also proposed to reform the EU migration policy, to strengthen the Schengen area through the co-management of migration policy at the European borders, and, particularly, the reform of the Dublin Agreement in order to move in the direction of a multispeed Europe.

The March 2018 elections represented a watershed for Italian democracy. It will be difficult for the winners to form a government because of the deep rivalries between their leaderships. But it will also be impossible for the losers to advance their program. In this stalemate, Italy will not be in the condition to contribute effectively to the debate on the reform of the eurozone. While the variegated anti-EU coalition has no clear strategy, the division of the country will make it the de facto southern offshoot of the Visegrád group. Thus, Italy will not exit from the EU, but it might contribute to the others' efforts to hollow out the EU from within.

Latvia's Future in a Deepened EU: Fine with the Right Wine

Karlis Bukovskis and Aldis Austers

Geopolitical considerations continue to define Latvia's foreign policy priorities, including Latvia's strategic positioning in relation to and within the EU. Economic and social convergence is also among the drivers behind Latvia's persistence to stay in the core of the EU. Latvia's public opinion shows high levels of support for the membership, and none of the notable political forces are positioning the country to exit the EU. Officially, Latvia stands for a strong union of independent states. In line with this, Latvia has been an ardent supporter of deepening the single market and the Economic and Monetary Union (EMU). However, Latvia has shown little appetite to see integration in such areas as taxation and social protection standards. In Latvia's view, deepening in these areas would infringe upon the country's economic competitiveness, coherent economic development, and productivity-based wage increases. Should there be a motion towards greater unity in sensitive areas, Latvia's acceptance would be conditional on either adequate compensatory mechanisms or a strong commitment from other EU member states to help each other when in serious trouble. Equal political and economic standing of the member states

K. Bukovskis (✉) • A. Austers
Latvian Institute for International Affairs, Riga, Latvia
e-mail: karlis.bukovski@liia.lv

M. Kaeding et al. (eds.), *The Future of Europe*,
https://doi.org/10.1007/978-3-319-93046-6_17

within the EU is of paramount importance to Latvia. Hence, a multi-speed Europe with objectively unsolvable differentiation tied to the economic, geographical, or cultural areas in the short term should be avoided at all costs.

Deeper Single Market, EU, EMU and Social Union

Latvia traditionally has been open-minded about liberal trade policies. Latvia is relatively weak in traditional industries. However, its strength is related to the services sector and new industries, e.g. in the digital area. Unfortunately, these strengths cannot be translated into sustainable economic success because the rules of the European single market largely do not apply to these areas, and many restrictions to cross-border transactions remain in place. Therefore, the Single Market Strategy, the Digital Single Market, the Capital Markets Union, the Banking Union, and the facilitation of labour mobility have to be promoted from Latvia's perspective, because these initiatives facilitate the country's competitive edge and embody the highest promise to complete economic and social convergence with the most affluent EU countries. Continuing to be dependent on energy imports from Russia, Latvia also places high hopes in the Energy Union.

In the context of the completion of the EMU, uniform benchmarks must be set for eurozone member states on the level of socio-economic development, i.e. legally binding convergence requirements, while allowing countries to follow their individual economic policies. A post of a Commissioner for internal economic convergence could be established to facilitate this.

To aid intra-sectoral competition without instigating intra-member state competition in the EU, two aspects can be useful: more intense collaboration when drafting national budgets and mandatory quotas in public procurement. The first implies regular annual visits by the European Commission and fellow eurozone parliamentarians to discuss the upcoming year's fiscal policy with the budgetary committees of the national parliaments. This peer review process would stimulate collaboration between national parliaments and EU institutions, provide additional intellectual input during budgetary procedures, and stimulate coherence among national budgets. The second aspect – mandatory quotas of 1% for each member state's businesses in national procurement procedures – would allow companies from smaller EU countries to gain greater EU-wide presence and increase competition, and thus quality, in national procurements.

The next major challenge of both the EU and the EMU is dealing with the complexity of the EU. Public understanding and trust in the EU requires that EU bodies and posts be consolidated and institutions be renamed. Submerging the Committee of Regions as a consultative body into the European Parliament would be the first step. Bureaucratic names that do not provide a clear understanding of the functions and institutional place of a body, like the European Stability Mechanism, European Union Military Staff, Permanent Structured Cooperation, and European Fiscal Board, should be changed. Using terms like "Department of" or "EU minister of" should finally become a norm after 60 years of integration. The same stands for posts. The existing proposal for the Commission President to draft agendas and chair meetings of the European Council would not distort the intergovernmental character of the latter. The EU treaties already state that there needs to be a reduction in the number of Commission members. Hence, having a list of the highest EU level political figures (presidents of the European Parliament, Commission, European Council, European Central Bank, Eurogroup, and commissioners as well as the High Representative) equal to the number of the EU member states would facilitate collaboration.

The social issues in Latvia have only recently become salient due to the high level of youth emigration from Latvia. Latvian businesses and liberal-minded circles object to creating a more generous social system on the pretext that it would compromise the competitiveness of Latvian exports, whose competitiveness is dependent more on low labour costs than on factor productivity. In the circumstances of increased social competition among the member states, it is in society's interests that the national social policies are also Europeanized. Like monetary sovereignty under free capital movement, labour market regulation at the national level under free movement of labour also becomes ineffective. At the same time, the costs of protecting the unemployed and seniors would still be carried by individual member states, which undermines public finances. To dissuade countries from following distortive taxation practices, a Social Union should also include a fiscal solidarity component. An EU-wide unemployment insurance scheme would entail a step towards that. Otherwise, mandatory standardisation in social policies and wages can be put in place once the country reaches the level of 95% of GDP per capita of the EU average.

Lithuania and the EU: Pragmatic Support Driven by Security Concerns

Ramūnas Vilpišauskas

State of Play

Lithuania has been focusing on several European policy priorities since its accession in 2004: support for reforms and closer relations between Eastern neighbours and the EU, completing its infrastructural integration with particular attention paid to energy and transport networks between the Baltic States and the remaining EU (Northern and Central Europe), dealing with so called 'left-overs' from accession, membership in the Schengen area and the eurozone, and economic convergence with the rest of the EU.

Some of these priorities have advanced significantly. For example, Lithuania joined the Schengen area in late 2007. Accession into the eurozone failed in the first attempt in 2007 due to its expansionary fiscal policy and the country's high inflation rates, but it succeeded in 2015. After a decade or more of delays resulting from political changes in ruling coalitions, major regional energy projects such as the Nord-Balt electricity link

R. Vilpišauskas (✉)
Institute of International Relations and Political Science, Vilnius University, Vilnius, Lithuania
e-mail: ramunas.vilpisaukas@tspmi.vu.lt

M. Kaeding et al. (eds.), *The Future of Europe*,
https://doi.org/10.1007/978-3-319-93046-6_18

between Lithuania and Sweden as well as the Lit-Pol link between Lithuania and Poland have become operational in 2015 and 2016. In terms of economic convergence, Lithuania has been one of the fastest converging economies during its first decade in the EU, reaching 75% of GDP per capita of the EU average in 2016 from around 53% in 2005. Fast convergence has, however, contributed to inflation rates above the eurozone average, which makes price increases the most important issue to Lithuanians recently, according to the Eurobarometer.

In other EU capitals, Lithuania has become mostly known for its focus on the Eastern neighbourhood (Eastern Partnership since 2009). The country's authorities have maintained continuity in terms of their strategic goals to promote closer relations between Eastern neighbours and the EU, to support reforms in those countries by providing technical and financial assistance, and to act as a political advocate of those countries in the EU and other international organisations. This type of policy also acts more broadly as an insurance policy against Russia, especially because of the country's aggressive policies towards Georgia and Ukraine.

There is a strong consensus among parliamentary political parties regarding Lithuania's EU membership and its European policy priorities, which also reflects popular support for the EU. Although it has been fluctuating since Lithuania's accession, it has been consistently higher than the EU average. Security concerns are one of the specific features of support for the country's membership in the EU, which coincides with strong support for NATO membership. Freedom of movement inside the EU is another important benefit to Lithuanians. However, the large numbers of migrants who left Lithuania for the UK, Ireland, and other EU member states have turned the topic of migration into one of the most controversial issues of public policies.

Takeaways

Emigration has become one of the most politically salient issues. Beyond that, the debate on how the country should prepare for decreased EU funding has started. These issues, together with concerns regarding the security situation in the Eastern neighbourhood, dominate the current political agenda in the country. The first two issues should be dealt with by completing education, health care, public administration, and pension reforms, which have been only partly undertaken since the transition started in the 1990s. At the same time, Lithuania should continue playing an active role in supporting reforms in Eastern Partnership countries because it has the credibility and expertise required for such a role.

Lithuanian authorities have been relatively silent on how they view ideas to reform the EU. The Lithuanian President has only stressed that she does not support a change of the EU Treaty. Furthermore, in the field of defence cooperation, Lithuania's main concern has been to preserve the key role of NATO and to avoid any possible duplication between NATO and the EU. This approach should be continued due to the crucial role the US plays in contributing to European security. The authorities were right to match their publicly voiced concern about the security situation with an increase in national spending on defence to reach 2% of the country's GDP in 2018. The arrival of Germany's military forces in Lithuania within the NATO framework is also a positive development, though an increase of anti-American attitudes in Germany and some other EU countries is a cause for concern.

On most other proposals regarding the reform of the eurozone, the Lithuanian position has been to suggest that the existing instruments can be put to better use and to wait for more concrete content of suggested reforms. Such a position indicates both possible flexibility in the negotiations and cautiousness expressed when privately drawing such 'red lines', which could be crossed in the future. However, keeping in mind Lithuania's traditional opposition to more integration in areas like corporate tax harmonisation, authorities would face a difficult dilemma between the political wish to be part of the core group of EU member states and national interests of economic competitiveness if such concrete proposals on further integration steps were brought onto the EU agenda.

A cautious attitude of Lithuanian authorities on eurozone reforms is understandable since it is based on the safeguard of sovereignty, which seemed to work during the Great Recession of 2009 when the country undertook fiscal adjustment measures without turning to external financial support and managed to recover relatively fast. The need to catch up economically and to further modernise the economy requires flexibility in economic policy making, including a tax regime favourable for investments. Debates on the next EU financial framework should be used as an opportunity to direct EU funding to more productive use and target those areas, which create European value added, especially taking into account Lithuania's geographical location and need to catch up.

Luxembourg and the EU: How to Integrate in the Face of Diversity

Anna-Lena Högenauer

A European Country

Luxembourg is one of the founding states of the EU and one of the most pro-European member states today. According to recent Eurobarometer surveys, 89% of Luxembourgers feel that they are 'citizens of the EU', and public support for key EU policies is higher than in any other member state: 96% of Luxembourgers are in favour of the free movement of citizens in the EU, and even after the years of crisis, 85% are in favour of a European Economic and Monetary Union with a single currency.

Some of this support can be traced back to pragmatic considerations: as one of the smallest member states, it depends on an open and integrated European economy for exports and imports. The free movement of citizens within the EU is vital too, as it allows the national economy to recruit a skilled workforce that cannot always be trained nationally: almost half of Luxembourg's inhabitants are foreigners (85% from the EU) and, in addition, 44% of the workforce are 'frontaliers' who live in Germany, Belgium,

A.-L. Högenauer (✉)
Institute of Political Science, University of Luxembourg,
Esch-sur-Alzette, Luxembourg
e-mail: anna-lena.hoegenauer@uni.lu

M. Kaeding et al. (eds.), *The Future of Europe*,
https://doi.org/10.1007/978-3-319-93046-6_19

or France and commute to Luxembourg. Politically, EU membership has allowed the country to punch above its weight class in international politics. Finally, Luxembourg has not only benefited from the presence of a number of EU institutions on its territory, but it has also recently done quite well when it comes to securing positions in the EU institutions.

These strong economic ties with Europe have also shaped the political landscape in Luxembourg. Thus, none of the political parties want to follow the British example and leave the EU. Rather, the two small euro-critical parties, the right-wing ADR and the left-wing Déi Lénk, want a different kind of EU. The ADR wants the EU to allow for more room for national sovereignty, and Déi Lénk wants more solidarity and less liberalism.

The support for integration goes occasionally even beyond pragmatic cost-benefit calculations. Luxembourg demands, for example, a stronger social pillar to support an Economic and Monetary Union – despite the fact that, as an economically strong member state, it would probably be a net contributor to such an initiative. Similarly, the government supports a common policy on migration (including a fairer distribution of refugees), despite the fact that the country has no external borders and therefore benefits from the current regime, whereby the burden lies in practice on Southern European countries. Of course, there are also some policy areas – such as corporate taxation – where Luxembourg is more defensive of its national interests.

Moving Forward as One or at Multiple Speeds?

The EU almost doubled in size (in terms of member states) through the Eastern enlargements since 2004. Under the influence of the eurozone and migration crises, the EU has become more divided in recent years. For Luxembourg, these tensions have resulted in a dilemma: on the one hand, the country is very pro-European. Its biggest party (the CSV) is in favour of a federal Union in the long term. It would therefore in principle like to see further integration by all member states. On the other hand, the tensions between member states mean that such a scenario is unrealistic.

In this situation, most Luxembourgish politicians prefer a multi-speed model of integration. Such a model would indeed be best for Luxembourg in the coming years. The risk is, of course, that a multi-speed EU becomes even more complex, and that those states that perform worst in a policy area opt out of integration because they are underperforming. However, the advantage is that the 'coalitions of the willing' can vary from policy to policy, and that all member states are likely to find something where they would like to lead the way. For Luxembourg, it means that the EU cannot be blocked by one or two reluctant states. As Luxembourg is usually strongly in favour of integration, it is likely to be one of the member states that are centrally involved in (almost) all integration projects. In concrete terms, it is one way for Luxembourg and the 'Digital 9' to move forward with the creation of a bigger European digital market that can compete with the US and Asia.

However, a multiple-speed approach does not work for all policy areas. For example, Luxembourg is adamant that the EU should have a common migration policy, especially for refugees, where all member states should be obliged to accept a certain number of refugees in their territory. This is seen as a crucial sign of solidarity with those Southern European countries that are the most severely affected by refugee streams. Not only does the government refuse to allow countries to 'opt out' of the burden-sharing, but it also advocates decision-making by majority vote rather than unanimity in order to prevent (selfish) national vetoes. Thus, the question is: who decides which policies are obligatory for everyone, and which can be handled in a multiple-speed model?

Another source of concern is Jean-Claude Juncker's suggestion to expand the eurozone to more Eastern European countries and the Schengen area to Romania and Bulgaria. Luxembourg's prime minister, Xavier Bettel, prefers to delay these expansions until the countries in question are ready, i.e. fulfil the criteria. This hesitation is wise in that the recent crises showed that major problems affect citizens' trust in the EU. It is more important to create policies that function than to create policies that are big.

Finally, Luxembourg faces an unusual dilemma over whether to replace the Chair of the Eurogroup, who currently reports to the Council of Ministers, with an EU finance minister who would be part of the Commission and report to the Parliament. Normally, Luxembourg is in favour of more influence for the Commission and the Parliament, but on this occasion, it is in its interest to defend the influence of the member states: Luxembourg has more influence in the Council than in the European Parliament. Also, once the Parliament gets a greater say in these matters, the control states have over taxation could erode – and taxation is one of the few national interests that Luxembourg vehemently defends. As in the case of Ireland, corporate taxation is seen as one of the competitive advantages of smaller states, and there is a reluctance to allow for harmonization on the European level. From a national perspective, it would thus be advisable to prevent the creation of an EU finance minister, and to give the Commission a bigger role in a European social pillar instead.

Malta: Small and Peripheral but Aiming for the Core of Europe

Mark Harwood

The First Decade of EU Membership

Malta is the smallest EU member state in terms of territory, population, and economy. Malta, in the centre of the Mediterranean, was a British colony until 1964, and its political and economic system bear a link to the British period. In the post-WWII drive to free the economy from its dependency on British military spending, successive governments cultivated tourism as well as manufacturing, in particular electronics and pharmaceuticals, as economic industries to bolster the country. In 1990, the Christian Democrats applied to join the EC with the issue of membership becoming divisive in this two-party state as the Socialists opposed. The issue was resolved in the 2003 EU referendum with a vote in favour, and Malta joined in 2004.

In contrast to the other Mediterranean member states, Malta's economy was not hard hit by the economic and financial crisis. More recently, the Maltese economy has flourished with growth rates in excess of the EU average and unemployment below 6%. Much of that economic success has

M. Harwood (✉)
Institute for European Studies, University of Malta, Msida, Malta
e-mail: mark.harwood@um.edu.mt

M. Kaeding et al. (eds.), *The Future of Europe*,
https://doi.org/10.1007/978-3-319-93046-6_20

been ascribed to a thriving financial service sector, an influx of e-gaming companies, growth in professional, scientific and technical activities as well as strong growth in tourism.

However, that success was also underscored by tensions in EU-Malta relations. An influx of irregular migrants via North Africa from 2002 brought Malta criticism for the conditions in which those migrants were housed while the EU was seen as failing to offer any assistance in managing migrant flows across the Mediterranean. More recently, revelations from the Panama Papers have led to calls from within the European Parliament and some member states for the Commission to investigate Malta's corporate tax system. The discord with the EU institutions in this area undermines the Government's stated aim of combatting tax harmonisation efforts at the EU level.

Ultimately, Malta has benefitted from EU membership and has done so in the face of core limitations, namely its size and limited influence, on the periphery of the continent and linked primarily to Italy, which continues to be preoccupied with domestic political problems, and the UK, which will soon leave the Union.

A Maltese Perspective on the Future of the EU

Despite the divisions amongst Maltese political parties on the question of EU membership in the 1990s, all major parties can now be termed Euro-enthusiasts. The Maltese population also shows high levels of support for Malta's place in the Union. Successive governments have made great efforts to keep Malta in the core group of integrated countries by joining the eurozone and Schengen area, returning to NATO's Partnership for Peace (to facilitate involvement in the Foreign Affairs Council), and participating in most areas of enhanced cooperation. In 2017, Malta completed its first stint as President of the Council of the EU and principally focused on migration flows in the central Mediterranean by holding an informal summit with all member states in Malta in February 2017.

While Malta is in favour of being a part of the core group of member states, it is clear that the idea of a federal Europe is unpalatable as no major political party espouses a United States of Europe. That said, it seems clear that an EU which provides greater economic and physical security to its members, underpinned by the value of solidarity, appears to be the best way forward for Malta. This can be best addressed by reforming the Union's institutions and policy scope.

In terms of reforming the EU political system, legitimacy is not a problem as Euroscepticism is low and turnout for EP elections is exceptionally high. Empowering the EP further makes little sense from a narrow, national perspective, because Malta will always have a limited place in the EP. Therefore, maintaining the centrality of the Council of the EU remains a keen interest. While Malta's voice is limited, it far outweighs its population size in areas that require unanimity or simple majority. The Commission, on the other hand, could be streamlined. The Commission is a principal actor for small states by providing expertise. Its decline relative to the other institutions can be countered by making the college smaller and simplifying its core activities. While the loss of a Commissioner might impact small states more, ensuring that Commissioners are rotated equally amongst member states seems a price worth paying for a more efficient Commission.

In terms of policy, the Union's increased competence is a benefit to Malta. A small state with limited expertise benefits from the EU's more technical policies. That said, a recent push into the area of defence cooperation and tax harmonisation could pose serious problems for Malta. In terms of defence cooperation, the initiative has a silver lining in that Malta, a neutral state, borders North Africa but depends on soft neutrality to defend itself. While joining a Cold War entity such as NATO would be impossible, joining an EU-led common defence initiative would be more probable. In this area, Malta has the most to contribute to the Union's future development; A Union better engaged in the Mediterranean will lead to greater regional stability, and Malta has long seen itself as a bridge in the region with established links to North African states. A Union active in securing a stable North Africa will benefit from Malta's contacts in the region.

Less promising is the Union's push towards tax harmonisation. Malta utilises its corporate tax system as a means to attract investment and compensate for the disadvantages of being a small, peripheral state. As the economy is increasingly dependent on financial services and niche industries such as e-gaming, any change in the country's tax system would be negative. Ultimately, a central preoccupation in Malta is the negative connotation of an EU where one-size-fits-all and where countries are denied the flexibility needed to deal with the reality of their size and location.

It is only by remaining at the core of the integrated countries that Malta can ensure that EU policies accommodate its needs, and this will come at a price. Ultimately, it is clear that Malta's interests centre on the Union doing more to ensure security within the Union and the Mediterranean and receptive to the individual needs of each of its member states, which can best be defended through the Commission and the Council.

The Netherlands and the EU: Strengthening but Not Centralising the EU

Adriaan Schout

Recent Sharpening in the Dutch EU-Tone

Despite its shifting reputation from a relatively supportive to a more eurosceptic country, the Netherlands has been pragmatic and constructive throughout the euro and the migration crises. Some issues stand out from the Dutch debates: the EU is of fundamental importance for economic and security reasons, and the euro needs to be stabilized. Although sometimes met with serious reservations, the Netherlands pragmatically supported Juncker's ambitious investment plans (the European Fund for Strategic Investments [EFSI]), the rescue mechanisms (the European Financial Stability Facility [EFSF] and European Stability Mechanism [ESM]), and strengthening the Commission's economic supervisory roles. In addition, the Netherlands was one of the major architects of the 'Turkey deal' on migration.

Nevertheless, the Dutch government recently had to take on a more defensive tone in response to, among others, Juncker's monumental ambitions for fixing the roof when the sun shines, Macron's ambitions for

A. Schout (✉)
EU Programme, Clingendael - Netherlands Institute of International Relations, The Hague, Netherlands
e-mail: aschout@clingendael.nl

M. Kaeding et al. (eds.), *The Future of Europe*,
https://doi.org/10.1007/978-3-319-93046-6_21

political eurozone governance, Schulz' (SPD) emphasis on 'the Ever-Closer Union and those who do not want it should leave', and rejuvenations of French-German opaque and ambitious leadership. Recently, the Dutch government organized a Northern alliance with eight countries to temper the ambitions of the European Monetary Union (EMU) and the EU-budget. Moreover, in spite of the more traditional preference for a pragmatic approach to roll with the punches, Prime Minister Mark Rutte felt challenged to also give an EU speech, in response to among others Macron, outlining his (sober) vision on the EU and on deeper integration of the eurozone. In fact, the Netherlands has been challenged to publicly commit itself to a (politically dangerous) redline: 'No transfer Union'.

In general, the Dutch prefer a confederal model of European integration based on the assumption that a strong EU can only be built on strong member states. Rutte therefore pleaded for reforms not so much at EU level but at the member state level so that countries can stand on their own feet. The eurozone will have 19 shock absorption mechanisms if member states respect the 60% rule (and if the Commission enforces it). Similarly, the need for a larger EU budget, an EU investment plan, or for an EU-type of IMF does not find much support, but they could be pragmatically accepted if only member states had sound track records in reforming their economies. Moreover, if ambitious proposals are put forward by the Commission, they should be accompanied by well-crafted impact assessments that include assessments of needs and alternatives. The recent Commission proposals for an EMU minister and European Monetary Fund (EMF) lack impact assessments, and they therefore reflect the mere political preferences of the Commission (or even a political power-grab). They cannot be regarded as well-argued policy initiatives that include careful attention for subsidiary and other better regulation criteria.

In terms of institutional development, the Dutch government (and probably the Dutch public at large) are reserved when it comes to *spitzenkandidaten* or strengthening the European Parliament with the power of the purse (taxation). The 'Ever-Closer Union' is not supported much nor is there a broadly-shared recognition for why deeper integration is needed if member states respect the agreements which they signed. By the same token, risk sharing in a banking union would probably be pragmatically accepted if only the banking union were based on solid rules, supervision and clarity that those who gain from risks also carry the burdens ('bail-in'). The current state of banking in the EU is simply not regarded as ready for risk sharing. Finally, Juncker's suggestions for EU enlargement would allow even more fundamentally weak member states to join.

A New Dutch Position in the EU?

The Dutch EU strategy is not just a response to ambitious widening and deepening EU agenda's. Power balances are changing between member states and between the EU institutions. With Brexit, the Netherlands loses a traditional alley and one of its defence mechanisms against overly ambitious French-German integration plans. More worrying is that, despite initial hopes for an effective First Vice-President, Frans Timmermans, the European Commission has become more political whereas the Netherlands has traditionally banked on a technocratic Commission that would supervise rules. The Commission is no longer 'our best friend'. Hence, the Dutch government is now reflecting on ways to build and even lead new – permanent or variable – coalitions.

Some expect the Netherlands to take over the awkward – obstructionist - position the UK occupied and some countries even indicated that they would hope for the Netherlands to assume a British style role. However, it is unlikely that the Netherlands will step into the UK's shoes. It is more likely that the government will explore the position of the 'bigger of the smaller' and assemble support from other countries to find a more receptive ear from the French-German axis and the EU Commission.

What Does This Say about the Netherlands as EU Partner?

This EU discourse in the Netherlands on strategies and coalition building should not be seen as Eurosceptic. The BBC posed the question: 'Will Dutch follow Brexit with Nexit?' (7 July 2016). The Financial Times (30 May 2011) presented the Netherlands as the 'most obstructionist' country. Despite its worries and reputation, the Netherlands has consistently ranked among to most-pro EU member states. Being a small open economy, the importance of European integration and the euro are deeply embedded in the Dutch narrative. The EU has become more debated and, hence, more politicized. This is a normalisation of European integration as a political theme.

Conclusions

The Dutch case leads to four points of reflection. First, the debates suggest a need for moderation in EU ambitions. Our countries are internally divided when it comes to the widening and deepening of the EU and eurozone. Brexit, the divided political landscape in Macrons France, loss of support for the GroKo in Germany, the fragmented political landscape in Italy, and other examples seem to call for moderation and not for the "radical centrism" now preached by, among others, Juncker and Macron. Second, the question needs to be asked whether the emphasis on 'more Europe' should be shifted towards 'better member states'. The need to deepen integration and the calls for a political union result from the weaknesses of individual member states. Hence, if countries reform, deeper integration is not needed, and the distinction between the euro-ins and the euro-outs becomes less pronounced. Third, it is remarkable that a critical debate, such as in the Netherlands, is often presented as 'Eurosceptic'. The EU is mature enough to handle criticism. Finally, the current debates signal that the EU Commission is losing formal support – and that is a serious issue. We urgently need a discussion on redesigning the Commission's tasks with a view to separating policy inputs, political decisions, monitoring, and enforcement. We not only need better member states, we also need better European checks and balances (i.e. separation of functions) and, hence, a better Commission.

Exit, Voice, and Loyalty: Norway's Options

Ulf Sverdrup

Imagine that Albert O. Hirschman, the late political economist and intellectual, was asked to assess the developments in Europe and its future. How would he interpret the situation, and what would he have said?

My guess is that his response would have been as follows: In a situation when decision makers and voters feel that the quality of their community is decreasing, or fail to see the benefits of its achievements, they tend to either opt for "voice" or for "exit". "Exit" means withdrawing from the relationship, while "voice" means attempting to repair, reform, or improve the relationship. He would probably also have reminded us of the fact that these two strategies are interrelated. If "exiting" is easily available and the threshold for leaving is low, it means that it will be less likely that the "voice" strategy will be used. Similarly, if "voice" is ignored and reform attempts are regarded as impossible, "exit" becomes a more likely approach.

There is a third factor to the equation: "loyalty". A strong feeling of "loyalty" might reduce the likelihood of "exit" and increase the likelihood of "voice". While he might have been cautious of making recommendations, he could have added some final remarks on how "loyalty" can be built. The "exit" of some can be used to increase the "loyalty" and belonging among the ones who are left. In addition, "loyalty" can increase if

U. Sverdrup (✉)
Norwegian Institute of International Affairs, Oslo, Norway
e-mail: us@nupi.no

M. Kaeding et al. (eds.), *The Future of Europe*,
https://doi.org/10.1007/978-3-319-93046-6_22

citizens and decision makers feel that they can be seen and their "voice" heard, and if they experience that they are able to successfully reform.

Today the three M's in European politics are playing these different roles. French President Macron is clearly the leading protagonist for the "voice" strategy, the British Prime Minister May is the leading person for the "exit" strategy, and German Chancellor Merkel has been the person expressing the strongest "loyalty" and sense of belonging.

However, we should also know that there is no clear boundary between membership and non-membership in the EU. I write this piece from the viewpoint of Norway. Norway is in some sense special. She is clearly a European country, but she is not a member of the European Union. However, she is very closely associated and integrated with the EU and with European societies through a range of agreements. As such, she is both inside and outside at the same time.

During the Brexit process, there has been much more coverage of the "Norway model" than before, as the UK and the EU are looking for options on how to resolve the terms for leaving the EU, the transition agreements, and the possible future arrangements. It remains to be seen whether the EU and the UK can build on the Norwegian lessons and experiences and find inspiration to design a bespoke agreement that can work for all parties.

However, the true lesson from the Norwegian experience is a simple one: it is easy to "exit" from EU membership, and it is fairly easy to lose your "voice", but it is more difficult and also undesirable to escape and leave European cooperation and integration. There are also the lessons from Switzerland, Iceland, Liechtenstein, the countries in the Balkan region currently negotiating for membership, as well as Ukraine and Turkey. I would be surprised if the UK ended up without a rather close relationship with the EU.

As a non-member, Norway has no formal "voice" in the debate on the future of the EU. This is to be expected, and it is fully legitimate that a club needs autonomy. However, this does not mean that Norway has no views on the future of the EU. Instead, it has to act as a lobbyist.

As a big investor in Europe through its Government Pension Fund and as an integrated part of the Single Market, Norway has its views on many issues, ranging from specific legal acts to the general architecture of the EU. Norwegians in general would like to have a competitive, innovative, well-functioning, and safe EU with fair controls at the external borders.

Norwegians would support an EU that is more active on the global stage and support the EUs promotion of the SDGs. They would like to see a Europe that is clearly working in support of multilateralism and that develops a good working relationship with NATO but does not duplicate it. As to the design of the EU, the Norwegians would probably be reluctant to promote further supranational solutions, but instead support multi-speed solutions. As the UK is leaving the EU, Norway, like some of the other Nordic countries, will also have to look for new allies and partners on some of the issues on the EU agenda. As Germany is already the most important partner, it will probably become more important, and we might also see more coordination attempts among the Nordics.

Norway's limited "voice" in the EU should not be confused with having no voice or say on the future of Europe. The EU is certainly an important aspect of Europe, it has made a huge contribution to European unity, and it remains a formidable gravitational force. But Europe is still something more as it relates to a bigger space, a way of living, values, culture, arts, history, etc. Most would agree that being European is something more than being an EU citizen.

There are also good reasons to believe that non-members can contribute to developing Europe in the future. For instance, The Norwegians, together with the other Nordic countries, constitute a small part of the European population, but in terms of the size of their economies they are not insignificant. More importantly, these economies have demonstrated that it is possible to be successful and competitive in global markets and to ensure a good and fair distribution of the benefits of globalization. The key solutions that the Nordics would advocate for in Europe is that taxation and flexible labour markets, combined with access to education and healthcare, are critical factors for building sustainable societies and economies in a competitive environment.

Our common challenge, as both outsiders and insiders, is therefore to recognize the multifaceted nature of Europe and to encourage non-members not to disengage from Europe while, at the same time, encouraging the EU to relate to its European partners outside the EU.

There are also some powerful but rather mundane processes of everyday life that might pull members and non-members apart. Exiting the EU implies less everyday encounters and exchanges, fewer partnerships, less shared information, and fewer shared perceptions. Outsiders will even disappear from the statistical tables and charts.

There is therefore a genuine risk that outsiders and insiders will gradually drift apart, and that non-members will be less engaged in, less capable of, and less committed to shaping the future of Europe. It might seem paradoxical, but if one has decided to exit, it might very well be that the country will be required to have even more loyalty to Europe to acquire a genuine and influential voice.

Solidarity with Poland but Not from Poland

Zdzisław Mach

The recent refugee crisis generated perhaps the most serious debate in the EU for many years, which touched upon the half-forgotten question of European values. Perhaps not quite unexpectedly, it was Eastern Europe that made it clear that Europe must again reflect on the very foundations of its integration and on what it means to be European. The value of solidarity came to the fore.

Paradoxically, Poland often speaks of the importance of the value of solidarity. The Polish government often calls for European solidarity when it has problems with Russia or when it fears potential security threats. Poland also expects continuous financial support from the EU in the name of solidarity with poorer, deserving countries. But when Mediterranean countries called for solidarity to help them cope with the inflow of refugees, the right-wing Polish government refused (even if the previous, more liberal government had agreed to accept a small number of refugees). This decision was a refusal of solidarity with refugees and also with other EU member states. It showed that Poland did not see itself as a member of the European community in any other sense than the common market and perhaps some other policies that bring immediate benefits to the country.

Z. Mach (✉)
Institute for European Studies, Jagiellonian University, Kraków, Poland
e-mail: zdzislaw.mach@uj.edu.pl

M. Kaeding et al. (eds.), *The Future of Europe*,
https://doi.org/10.1007/978-3-319-93046-6_23

A feeling of belonging to a community of European countries, or what should be called European identity, has always been a problem in Poland. In spite of frequent declarations of "returning to Europe" after decades of communism, for most Poles the EU remains an external entity, a foreign power. EU institutions are seen as alien, and if they comment or criticize developments in Poland they are accused of intruding upon internal affairs of a sovereign country. It is interesting to observe that this is exactly the same language that the communist governments used in reaction to criticism from the West. The well-known support of the majority of Poles for membership in the EU is real, but it is exclusively linked to financial gains and not to a sense of community or attachment to European values. Europe is "them" not "us", as one can hear every day in the media. Europe is like Santa Claus: liked for bringing presents, but otherwise not interesting and not someone with whom to identify.

In its attempt to gain popularity, the present Polish government has developed a populist rhetoric of national independence, sovereignty, and pride, together with xenophobic and nationalistic attitudes not only towards refugees, but also any cultural "others". The Polish nation is seen as a community of tradition, language, and Roman Catholicism, speaking with one voice and sharing the same conservative world-view and way of life. Cultural others and foreign (especially liberal) values are seen as a danger to the Polish national identity. This also makes the EU foreign because of the values that it represents. The Polish government's current attempts to secure a monopoly of power consist of the elimination of all barriers that prevent the authorities from creating a new, illiberal democracy supported by the majority of society but not controlled by domestic liberal institutions, free media, NGOs, an independent judiciary, or by EU institutions. The EU is therefore perceived as an obstacle in this process of building an illiberal, authoritarian system.

What, then, is the future of Poland in the EU and its contribution to the Community? Under the present government, Poland is not likely to support any further integration. It will also move away from European standards regarding liberal democratic principles and procedures as well as European values. Paradoxically, the main if not the only contribution that Poland is now offering to Europe is to make Europeans aware of the importance of values. Many took values such as the rule of law for granted and assumed that they could no longer be questioned. Poland and Hungary show that this is not the case. To preserve its identity, Europe must stand by its values more firmly and consistently. Financial assistance should be given only to those who adhere to European liberal values. Breaking treaties, European law, or basic freedoms on which European integration is based should result in exclusion from the community. European treaties must be respected and enforced. Solidarity should be given to those who are prepared to offer solidarity to others. If, as an effect, some member states have (or decide) to leave the community, then it will be better for Europe. It is better to integrate with those who share the same values than to dilute the community of values by accepting reluctant members.

To prevent such a radical development and to keep Poland in the community, liberal forces in the country, assisted by EU institutions, must launch a campaign of education and identity building to make more Polish citizens familiar with European liberal values and to convince them of their importance in maintaining a free society. Education is where most efforts must be made to develop European identity among young Poles. It seems that this area was disregarded in past years, which led many young people to have little sense of belonging to the common European community. A European perspective and a European frame of reference ought to be developed in various subjects taught at school.

Beyond that, the political opposition and liberal opinion leaders should firmly stand by European values consistently emphasizing their significance as the foundation of a common European identity and the condition of belonging to the European community. Information about the benefits of EU membership should be linked to the image of Europe as a social, political, and cultural community. A realistic road map leading to the introduction of the European common currency should be drawn and promoted, in view of the fact that the majority of Polish people are afraid of the euro as they expect a rapid increase of prices. And, what has become increasingly more important recently, all alternative proposed forms of supranational integration, such as Visegrád, 16+1 (proposed by the Chinese as a form of cooperation between former communist countries), or the Three-Seas idea of connecting countries of Central and Eastern Europe should be presented as proposals that aim to divide and destroy the EU.

Without more identification with liberal European values and without more European identity, which can coexist with national identity rather than being seen as its alternative, Poland will find it difficult to remain in an integrating Europe in the long term.

The Bell Has Rung: Portugal's Main Bet Is on the Conclusion of the EMU

Alice Cunha

On one of his last visits to Brussels, Prime Minister António Costa claimed that 2017 was "a particularly tasty year for Portugal". Well, Salvador Sobral won the Eurovision song contest, Cristiano Ronaldo was awarded his fifth Ballon d'Or, and Mário Centeno was elected Eurogroup president. But what about a serious discussion on European Union matters? And the country's inputs on several matters? Besides the usual public speeches on "our place" in Europe, "30 years of membership" and others related to current 'crises', such as those on refugees and populism (two "no" problems in Portugal), no proper or serious discussion is being held in the country, even after the European Commission's White Paper on the Future of Europe. Obviously, the Minister for Foreign Affairs pointed out which scenarios were convenient for the country and which ones were not. The Prime Minister even tweeted that this document was a "good start for an indispensable debate", but the beginning of the debate is still to be seen at the governmental level. If it weren't for two series of conferences organised by civil society, no discussion on the present and future of the EU or and the country would have been had.

A. Cunha (✉)
Institute of Contemporary History, NOVA University, Lisbon, Portugal
e-mail: alice.cunha@fcsh.unl.pt

M. Kaeding et al. (eds.), *The Future of Europe*,
https://doi.org/10.1007/978-3-319-93046-6_24

Officially, two of the five scenarios clash with national interests. The second ("nothing but the single market") doesn't allow for the completion of the Economic and Monetary Union (EMU), and it also pushes back progress in social and fiscal policies. The fourth ("doing less more efficiently") aims at improving in some areas (such as security and foreign policy) at the cost of others, namely employment and cohesion. The favourite scenario is the last one ("doing much more together"), since it would allow the EMU to conclude, adding a financial capacity to it.

Although European integration is a fairly contentious subject between the two major parties that compete for office (Socialist and Social Democrat), the two left wing parties that support the Government in Parliament (Communist and Left Bloc) do not share the same vision. They even have completely different positions regarding the EU's future and point out Europe's current failures. The Communists want to renegotiate the public debt and free Portugal from "the euro's submission" and EU's impositions and constraints; the Left Bloc argues in favour of debt restructuring as well as the nationalisation of strategic companies. To a certain extent, however, this is more the need of an ideologically assertive strategy rather than a real action plan.

Against this backdrop, and despite the fact that migration, security, and defence have been imposed as unavoidable priorities in the debate on the future of Europe, the Portuguese Government almost only talks about the deepening, consolidation, and conclusion of the EMU, arguing that without completing it there will not be a solid foundation on which to build Europe's future. On January 12, 2018, the Portuguese Minister of Finances, Mário Centeno, took office as Eurogroup president and now has two and a half years to give his/Portugal's contribution to the achievement of that goal. In particular, he will strive to make the budgetary capacity of the eurozone based on its own resources, which would enable investments, eliminate structural barriers to competitiveness, and strengthen growth. It may also ensure the stability of the single currency union and help member states weather economic shocks. Another priority is the strengthening of the Banking Union, which includes improvements in the Single Resolution Fund and the European Deposit Insurance Scheme.

As part of a new "southern front", whose leaders met in Rome in early January, Portugal may also influence EU policy making on other issues such as migration, social equality, and employment. In the first case, Portugal could call for a common European migration policy that prevents irregular flows and also addresses the root causes of mass migration. The country could also call for a fairer Common European Asylum System, which respects the principles of responsibility and solidarity of all, especially towards frontline member states. Regarding social equality, the Portuguese position is that there must not be a division between a 'Europe of competitiveness' and a 'Europe of cohesion', as the Cohesion Policy must evolve to combine territorial cohesion and responses to its main beneficiaries (people) by being linked to the social pillar of the EU and addressing demographic, labour, and inclusion challenges that confront European societies today.

The Portuguese Empire has long been gone, and its EU membership is solid. Overall, Portugal is currently in favour of the Digital Single Market, the Energy Union and joint climate actions, the Banking Union, and everything else that pushes the EU forward and enables the country to be at the forefront of European integration. Past and present costs are still significant. Yet, and even in the most difficult period of the Adjustment Programme when Europe-wide indicators of public trust in European institutions fell, Portuguese membership in the EU was never questioned by any important sector of Portuguese society. After the EU bailout, the country has been recovering economically and seeking to forget the stigma of the troika intervention, both internally and externally. At the same time, the country calls for policies that promote economic growth and social wellbeing. But it is still a small, poor, and peripheral country in an increasingly differentiated and asymmetric EU. Nevertheless, and despite its predominant EU membership, Portugal has a universal foreign policy – which is rare for a small country – and, in reality, the vectors of its foreign policy (the Atlantic, Africa, Latin America, the Community of Portuguese Speaking Countries) – add real value to the EU, both economically and geo-strategically.

Portugal has managed to belong to the core of European integration, namely the Schengen area and the eurozone, and more recently PESCO. If the past illustrates the future, no radical change of position is to be expected, and Portugal will continue to be committed to the European integration process, despite the fact that the country hasn't really had a strategy towards the EU since its accession request. The country has always had a position towards different topics, but it remained stuck in the "good pupil" approach. In fact, from the very beginning that Portugal was considered as the "good pupil" of European integration, that "stigma" has never really left the country.

The EU's Young and Restless Democracy: Romania's Lessons and Contribution

Bianca Toma

Romania will host a special summit dedicated to the future of the European Union in Sibiu on May 9, 2019 after the United Kingdom will have left the Union. It is a moment when, as announced by the European Commission's President Jean Claude Juncker in his speech on the state of the EU (2017), EU leaders are expected to take the necessary decisions for a more united, stronger, and democratic Europe. The five scenarios on the future of the EU launched by Brussels were not received with much enthusiasm in Bucharest, as President Klaus Iohannis announced that he does not support the multispeed Europe. 2019 will also be the year when, for the first time, Romania will hold the rotating presidency of the Council of the Union.

Key roles lie ahead for one of the EU's youngest democracies. And in order to understand what is at stake for Romania, what kind of roles it would like and, more importantly, it is able to assume, one needs to have a brief overview of the challenges the country is currently facing: Romania is going through a time of political turbulence that may lead to a significant step backwards with regard to the major institutional reforms achieved in its 10 years of European integration. Moreover, taking a closer look at

B. Toma (✉)
Romanian Centre for European Policies, Bucharest, Romania
e-mail: bianca.toma@crpe.ro

M. Kaeding et al. (eds.), *The Future of Europe*,
https://doi.org/10.1007/978-3-319-93046-6_25

what happened in Poland, after Warsaw's successful legislative changes affecting the judiciary, we've got a stronger wave of Euro-antipathy now that Brussels has been painted as an enemy of the country by Polish politicians. The pattern has already been adopted by local Romanian politicians and assertive media outlets. Romanian politicians have pointed out the top European Commission leaders, while bureaucrats or MEPs criticizing Bucharest's actions are often labelled, as in Poland, "traitors".

The stalemate in Bucharest is generated by anticorruption prosecutors' blocked investigations, which have been stalled to the benefit of the leaders of the majority coalition in the Parliament (PSD ALDE). The head of the main government party (PSD), Liviu Dragnea, is accused of corruption and abuse of power in several investigations. The latest allegations also point to the fraudulent use of European funds. As he didn't succeed in quickly amending the criminal laws and the provisions on corruption offences to his and other influential Romanian politicians' favour, the PSD leader withdrew his political support from his own government twice within one year. Bucharest now has its third government in less than 12 months. Nevertheless, civil society stood firmly in favour of upholding the rule of law: the judiciary retaliated and resisted the political assault, and hundreds of thousands of citizens protested with EU flags in their hands.

Despite the political turmoil, Romania had one of the highest economic growth rates in the EU in 2017 – 6.7%, according to the EC's estimation. Future forecasts remain optimistic, but more moderate growth is to be expected. Analysts warn, however, that a number of controversial social measures like salaries, pension increases, and very low absorption of European funds are also likely to significantly affect the budgetary balance.

Romanian's Contribution

With a public agenda full of political tensions, coupled with populist rhetoric and nationalist accents, there is little time for substantive debates on the role of the EU in Romania and the region, on the lessons Romania learned and can share within the region, and on its role in shaping the future of the EU. Ambitions are realized at the last minute, and potential alliances are not formed because of institutional instability.

However, there are undeniable areas in which Romania can play an important role in the future of the EU.

First, Romania can provide a response to the breakdown of democracy in some member states. The response can stem from Romanians' pro-European enthusiasm, in contrast to Western self-sufficiency or apathy. Political correctness and European technocracy have prevented Brussels from encouraging hundreds of thousands of Eastern Europeans who came out with flags in their hands in recent unprecedented protests. There have been many voices in various member states stating that Brussels did not know how to give a fitting emotional response to Romanians' determination to defend the EU and its values. It is also not clear whether the EU takes them into account when rewriting the future of the EU or when it reposes political solutions to the assaults on democracy and the rule of law in some member states. Civil society in these countries are increasingly valuable assets to the EU's transformative power, and it shall be put to work for the future of the EU.

The lessons from Romania and Bulgaria's accessions are no reasons for the apathy of further enlargements. One can pinpoint integration and transition lessons which these countries, and also those that joined the EU in 2004, experienced that make them exemplary. No other country in Central and Eastern Europe has been more successful in responding systemically and extensively to arrears related to judicial reform and the challenges of endemic corruption, including high-level corruption, than Romania. Moreover, the reality of Romania's role as a pillar of stability on a regional level needs to be further strengthened. From this perspective, the financial and technical assistance provided by Romania to the Republic of Moldova has some success stories to share.

Romania is also engaged in strategic energy investments by consolidating its position in the field of energy security on a regional and, implicitly, European level. The exploration of Black Sea gas fields and the development of a regional energy corridor through a gas transport infrastructure project managed by the national company Transgaz (and co-funded by the EU) strengthen national energy independence and also connect the country with its neighbours.

The most important energy infrastructure project, the Bulgaria-Romania-Hungary-Austria gas pipeline (the BRUA pipeline), was also initiated by the Romanian Transgaz and ensures the transport of natural gas from the Caspian region but also from other possible sources, including liquefied natural gas (LNG) from the United States. Through this infrastructure, gas will be able to reach all of Central Europe and thus greatly reduce its dependence on Russian gas. The first stage of this project is scheduled to be finished in December 2019 with concrete enlargement plans. Romania can and will claim a central role in the negotiations for and planning of the roles for the construction of the Energy Union and implementation of the EU's Energy Security Strategy.

While Romania hopes for a narrative on the future of Europe closer to the "More Together" scenario, the country needs to ambitiously work on building its alliances within the EU with the strengths of a successful transition experience and a pivotal status of stability in the Black Sea region.

Being European: The Slovak Way

Ol'ga Gyárfášová and Lucia Mokrá

Slovakia has achieved several milestones since its accession to the European Union in 2004, in the area of political discourse, perception of EU-membership, and also with regards to the performance of the country on the "European parquet". It was not clear at the end of the 1990s whether Slovakia would overcome its integration deficit and whether it would become a member of the western-democratic clubs with other post-communist countries. Slovakia had entered the EU with enthusiasm and the feeling that "we got it".

The positive mood continued throughout the first years of membership: in late 2006, 85% of respondents supported Slovakia's EU membership, findings which were also supported by Eurobarometer data. Even though the "honeymoon" phase from the first years of membership ended, Slovakia is still a pro-European country in the EU, and the EU agenda is considered to be an integral part of national politics.

Nevertheless, public attitudes changed during the "Greek crisis" as it reminded Slovak citizens that its EU membership does not only mean that it can receive EU funds, but that the country also needs to offer solidarity and to provide help to others. It escalated the position of political parties,

O. Gyárfášová (✉) • L. Mokrá
Faculty of Social and Economic Sciences, Comenius University in Bratislava, Bratislava, Slovakia
e-mail: olga.gyarfasova@uniba.sk; lucia.mokra@fses.uniba.sk

M. Kaeding et al. (eds.), *The Future of Europe*,
https://doi.org/10.1007/978-3-319-93046-6_26

and the European agenda was more intensively politicized in national political competition for the first time. In 2015 and 2016, the migration crisis became a central topic of the national parliamentary elections. Subsequently, the murder of an investigative journalist and his girlfriend at the beginning of 2018 triggered an unprecedented domestic political crisis. Slovakia experienced the biggest citizens′ protests since the Velvet Revolution in November 1989. On March 9, more than 120,000 people took to the streets. The political consequences for the country remain to be seen.

Concrete Recommendations for an Increased "Europeaness"

Although EU – Slovakia relations somehow fluctuate according to discussed topics and the concrete political agenda, they are still viewed as a positive win-win situation. There are, however, a few sets of recommendations which might help to strengthen the position of the country in the EU and sustain the positive public image of the EU within Slovakia:

a) The Slovak Republic used to be "evaluated" as a pro-European member, but formal legitimacy was rather weak. Slovakia had the lowest voter turnout out of all EU countries in its third elections for the European Parliament in 2014. It was repeatedly confirmed that there is a serious gap between satisfaction with EU membership and its performance on the one side and an active approach to "European issues" on the other side.

   We therefore consider it necessary to initiate and encourage a more intense discussion on the future of Europe in Slovakia. National leaders need to communicate proactively, objectively and transparently on EU matters, including both best practice examples and negative experiences. The focus should be placed on increasing voter turnout in the next European Parliament elections based on the information shared with the electorate, e.g. by promoting the participation of young people, employing alternative voting methods, or running campaigns on EU topics.

b) While EU membership is publicly viewed positively, EU topics are not always part of the national political parties' agendas. Until the fall of the government in autumn 2011, European topics did not play a major role in the formation of political parties' positions in Slovakia, as these were mainly on the periphery of interest. Political scientists also marked Slovakia as a "problematic candidate but loyal EU member". The later observation also led to an increase of Euroscepticism in the country.

The two main Eurosceptic parties in the country, the SNS (Slovak National Party) and the SaS (Freedom and Solidarity), mainly refer to the EU as an "enemy" and use the populistic approach of criticizing the EU without providing substantive arguments or proposing solutions. Their Eurosceptic attitudes, however, somewhat reflect the deteriorating public opinion on Slovakia's membership in the EU. The government, therefore, needs to transparently present all facts on EU matters and policies without misinformation or denigration.

c) Throughout recent years, migration has become the central topic not only in the EU, but particularly in CEE countries. Slovakia is characterized by cultural homogeneity, despite the relatively large portions of traditional autochthonous ethnic minorities. The country was not specifically touched by the increase of migration in the 20th century, with few experiences of incoming migration and connected issues of integration and inclusion. In June 2017, there were 97,934 foreigners registered in Slovakia, which represents only 1.8% of the whole population. While these numbers are considerably low, the proportions of foreigners have increased from 22,108 in 2004. Lower numbers of foreigners can only be found in Bulgaria (1.03%), Croatia (0.98%), Lithuania (0.65%), Romania (0.54%), and Poland (0.39%). Therefore, Slovakia's experience with foreigners is very low.

We therefore recommend that the Slovak government, which had elaborated on and already presented the principle of flexible solidarity in relation to migration during its EU presidency in the second half of 2016 (however without specific success on the European level), should focus on raising public's awareness of migrants and specifically refugees by providing explanatory campaigns, strengthening national offices' competencies and capacities when dealing with migrants and refugees; contributing to common EU migration work, e.g. the cooperation with Austria in 2015–2016 in providing shelters to asylum seekers until their status was adopted by national authorities; and cooperating on the creation of joint police teams in Greece under the EU mission. In this sense, the government should welcome closer cooperation with NGOs and other stakeholders.

Conclusion

In autumn 2017, Slovak membership in the EU was considered a good thing by 50% of the population. Even 74% were convinced that the country has profited from its membership.

The current leading governmental party Smer-SD had already exercised a rather ambitious pro-European rhetoric and politics. In recent discussions, it also became clear that Slovakia wants and also should belong to the core of the EU. Nevertheless, without clear steps or strategies, the current government's agenda remains vague and fact-based discussions on the pros and cons of EU membership exist practically only in academia.

This needs to change in order for the vision to belong to the core of EU integration to become a reality. It is high time for new dynamics in the national debate on the future of Europe.

Slovenia: From High Enthusiasm to Frustrating Indifference

Maja Bučar

Since Slovenia's independence in 1991, accession to the EU and NATO has been a key focus of the country's external politics. The 2003 referendum on EU membership received nearly 90% support. Yet this enthusiasm has dwindled over the years, and by 2017, only 45% of its citizens think that EU membership is a good thing for the country.

What happened? Who or what is responsible for such a change in attitude? Were the initial expectations set too high? Or had the practice of everyday politics, including the political blame placed on Brussels for so many of the hard-received reforms, fired back by creating a feeling among the public that Slovenia has not been getting a fair deal? The financial and economic crisis that began in 2008 hit the country hard, and even though most of the reasons for the deep crisis of the banking sector and the subsequent high budget deficit can be explained by delays and insufficient structural reforms, the need for strict financial consolidation was attributed to requests from Brussels. The experience with the refugee crisis in 2015 and the subsequent changes in border procedures with restrictions both to the north (Austria introduced additional border checking) as well

M. Bučar (✉)
Faculty of the Social Sciences, University of Ljubljana, Ljubljana, Slovenia
e-mail: Maja.Bucar@fdv.uni-lj.si

M. Kaeding et al. (eds.), *The Future of Europe*,
https://doi.org/10.1007/978-3-319-93046-6_27

as to the south (wired fence) additionally lowered the belief that the EU has an efficient common mechanism to address different crises.

One of the most important events, where Slovenians have high expectations from the EU, is the border settlement with Croatia. The arbitration ruling, issued by the UN Arbitration court on June 29, 2017, should have been implemented by the end of 2017. According to reports by the Slovenian media, the Commission supports the arbitration process and the Tribunal's ruling and expects both countries to do the same. This created the impression that Slovenia can count on additional help in negotiating its implementation with Croatia. By the end of the year, no progress had been achieved, yet Juncker issued a warning to the Croatian prime minister in the beginning of February that raised expectations that the Commission would become more actively involved. It remains to be seen how this will unfold, but there is little doubt that the public's opinion on the EU will be shaped by the role that the Commission plays in this case.

Looking at the Future of the EU

In spite of the relatively low score on the image of the EU, where only 34% of Slovenians see it positively and 46 neutrally, Slovenians believe that the EU should intervene more in several policy areas. Especially high expectations are placed in the area of economic policy: unemployment and tax fraud should be addressed more actively by the EU, according to 88% and 86% of the replies respectively. These positive replies are in sharp contrast to the very low interest in European affairs, where only 40% of respondents expressed interest in EU policy processes. Here, we believe, is the most important area where proactive national policy promoting the EU can assist in shaping its future.

Slovenian policymakers should use the period before the next Slovenian Council presidency to think about what kind of role Slovenia wants to play in the EU. Slovenia has neither the interest nor the capacity to deal with all EU policies, so it has increasingly become a passive observer of developments, hoping only that if more than a single-tier EU evolves, we don't have to settle for the second or third group.

Now it is important to carefully choose the most significant areas in which Slovenia can contribute at the EU level. This calls for an open discussion at home and a careful, honest evaluation of our potential. One of the problems might very well be the low level of expertise often found not only among the general public (which is not interested in EU policies), but also among politicians and the public administration. All political bodies underestimate the need to systematically build expertise on EU matters, which leads to suboptimal decisions or silent resignation to the opinions of others. Yet Slovenia could be a much more active member if properly organized.

One of the areas in which we could be more actively involved is the enlargement process. Even though there are signs of enlargement fatigue among EU members, Slovenia has a lot of interest in the continuation of membership negotiations with the Western Balkan countries. This area is of strategic economic, political, and security importance for the country. We have already initiated several activities in the past and have expressed our sincere interest in promoting the Europeanisation of these countries. By developing cooperations and other forms of technical assistance, Slovenia can help Western Balkan countries to align with the *acquis* as well as to adopt other EU standards. Yet, to convince other EU member states of our capability to act as a serious partner, we need to dedicate sufficient support to this policy focus continuously.

During its 2008 presidency of the EU Council, Slovenia launched the Ljubljana process in the area of EU research policy. Being (still) among the more successful EU13 countries when it comes to Horizon2020, Slovenia could focus on further developing its expertise in the research, development, and innovation (RDI) area to help less active countries close the gap in this field by promoting the design of special measures that favour the EU13. Slovenia successfully chaired EUREKA during the period of the launch of EUROSTARS and the formulation of the new EUREKA strategy, suggesting there is a sustained level of expertise available in the country in the field of RDI policy-making. Should this area be selected as one of Slovenia's priority areas for higher engagement at the EU policy level, this expertise could be further enhanced to benefit not only Slovenia and the EU, but also the EU13 and other less research oriented countries that are often forgotten in the dialogue among the top players in RDI.

To conclude, acting in a selected number of policy fields would improve Slovenia's role in the EU as well as increase the visibility of the EU in the country because a proactive role in Brussels would suggest to the public that even the voice of a small country can make a difference.

Spain in the EU: Eager to Regain Centrality

Ignacio Molina

Despite a recent recession, the period in which Spain has been a member of the EU has been the most stable, dynamic, and successful in the country's modern history. Consolidation of an advanced democracy, economic convergence with western countries, and a more influential foreign policy are developments inextricably connected with the country's Europeanisation. The EU is widely perceived as beneficial, supporting domestic governance. It is considered an essential part of the country's national narrative, following José Ortega y Gasset who argued already in 1910 that Spain itself was a problem and 'Europe its solution'.

Although indicators of public confidence in the EU suffered during the economic crisis, social support has recovered after 2014. The latest Eurobarometers show that Spaniards consider themselves citizens of the EU and are mostly in favour of the euro and common supranational policies on migration and defence. There is no Eurosceptic political party, even if the left-wing coalition IU-Podemos is critical of some EU decisions.

After a period in which Spanish politics and policies were somewhat "de-Europeanised", the EU has certainly returned to the centre. Today, the consensus on the ever-closer Union goal remains in place among

I. Molina (✉)
Elcano Royal Institute, Madrid, Spain
e-mail: imolina@rielcano.org

M. Kaeding et al. (eds.), *The Future of Europe*,
https://doi.org/10.1007/978-3-319-93046-6_28

the two big traditional parties, PP and PSOE, and the new liberal party Ciudadanos, which is currently leading the polls. The peripheral nationalists in the Basque Country and Catalonia also favour EU-integration, although in the latter case the enthusiasm is now much less evident due to the EU's position in support of the territorial integrity of Spain and its refusal to play any role in negotiations after the failed unilateral declaration of independence in the Catalan regional parliament.

It remains to be seen how the transformation from a two-party system to a much more fragmented political landscape will impact the Spanish EU policy making process which has been so far very dominated by the central executive. The new situation will not necessarily lead to the Parliament systematically blocking governmental initiatives, but rather to the need for building consensus.

In Search of a More Proactive Way

Spanish elites are concerned about their lost influence in Brussels. During the 1990s, Spain played an important role regarding, among other things, the creation of EU citizenship, a strong regional policy, counter-terrorism cooperation, and the heightened awareness of geographical priorities to the external EU agenda such as the Southern Mediterranean or, to a lesser extent, Latin America. However, it is more difficult to find examples of Spanish leadership, including relevant appointments to top EU jobs, after 2000, especially considering the combination of introspection and Eastern enlargement on top of the economic crisis.

The country's vulnerability reflects the damage a peripheral position within the EU can cause. Despite a federalist approach, Spain still shows a reactive attitude in Brussels. It must venture to do a lot more. Current circumstances seem favourable to regain centrality in the EU. With Brexit and strong Euroscepticism in Poland or Italy, Spain may benefit from the solid foundations of its European standards, the country's strong economic recovery, and its reinforced weight in EU institutions.

In the same vein, the country's potential for alliances is growing. Madrid has established annual meetings with Paris, Berlin, Rome, and even Warsaw throughout the last decades, and it now aspires to institutionalise a "Big Four" format of mini-summits with Germany, France, and Italy. In addition, Spain which traditionally enjoys dense bilateral relations with Portugal, has reinforced its co-operation with the Mediterranean EU countries through the new Southern European group. Finally, it has also augmented its attractiveness for mid-sized Northern member states, such as the Netherlands or Sweden, that are now seeking new European partners.

Policy-priorities can easily be identified: on the economic front, the completion of the Banking Union or mutualisation of debt. It is unclear if Spain will change its attitude towards the EU budget once it becomes a net contributor in the post 2020 Multiannual Financial Framework. However, it will continue to support a strong agricultural policy and cohesion fund, which will perhaps be less oriented towards infrastructures and more focused on youth employment. On the Digital Single Market agenda, Spain supports an ambitious EU policy regarding technology and societal change. Stronger energy interconnectivity via France and the fight against climate change are other top interests.

European management of the bloc's external borders is a main objective which takes into account the complex geographical position of the country. Linking control of illegal immigration and development cooperation in the emigrating countries, even if very controversial, has been considered a model for the EU during the refugee crisis.

Finally, Spain is unambiguously in favour of a larger role for the EU in world affairs. In most cases, with the notable exception of Kosovo's recognition, its foreign policy is aligned with the EU's external action. The two world regions in which Spanish diplomacy is more interested are Latin America and North Africa, where the country's energy supply, the fight against terrorism, and the control of migrant flows are high on the agenda. Despite its relatively low military spending, the country has been involved in all EU defence missions abroad.

Shaping the EU

Spain has significant comparative advantages in the EU policymaking process. While size matters, qualitative enhancers such as a globally spoken language, relative institutional and administrative stability, its committed Europeanism, and the firm place of its three biggest parties in the main European ideological families must also be taken into account. To reap the benefits of its strength, Spain could consider to (a) devise and defend its own integration story by identifying which Europe suits Spain; (b) creatively accommodate its national interest within the agenda of the EU institutions; (c) benefit from the quality and skills of Spanish representatives; and (d) improve coordination on a domestic level. Just putting the integration process at the heart of its national project is not enough. Spain must also dare to lead.

Managing the Risk of Periphery: Sweden and the Future of the EU

Göran von Sydow

Centripetal and centrifugal forces are simultaneously operating within the EU. While the eurozone states have tighter cooperation, several non-eurozone states are pondering what position to take in this new context. The Swedish aim has been to minimise divisions within the Union while simultaneously being loyal to the efforts made by the eurozone to save the currency. Furthermore, there is a considerable degree of hesitancy towards delegating authority to the European level over issues closely related to sovereignty. In sum, this calls for quite a delicate balancing act.

Since joining the EU in January 1995, Sweden has been closely allied with the UK in most aspects of European affairs. The logic of Swedish EU-membership was largely an instrumental one motivated by economic reasons. In a way similar to the UK, Sweden has had preferences which are critical of any major leaps towards a more federal Europe. Similar to the UK, Sweden has placed great emphasis on making the EU a well-functioning (internal) market that promotes economic efficiency. In general, the two countries have often shown reluctance towards any further delegation of authority to the supranational level, preferring instead to

G. von Sydow (✉)
Swedish Institute for European Policy Studies, Stockholm, Sweden
e-mail: goran.vonsydow@sieps.se

M. Kaeding et al. (eds.), *The Future of Europe*,
https://doi.org/10.1007/978-3-319-93046-6_29

promote intergovernmental or 'softer' modes of governance for the EU. Better regulation, a stronger role for national parliaments, and support for enlargement over a deepening of the EU have been areas of common agreement. It is therefore not surprising that Sweden has been the member state that most frequently voted like the UK in the Council and whose contact between the two countries' civil servants have been particularly intense.

The possible centrifugal stream that may come as a reaction to the deepening of the eurozone may affect the long-term role of non-eurozone countries such as Sweden. Public opinion remains solidly against joining EMU and has not changed drastically since the dramatic phase of the euro crisis in 2010. This will undoubtedly frame Swedish contributions to discussions concerning the future deepening of the EU. Public opinion is solidly in favour of EU-membership. Hence, the task is to ensure that the formula of full EU-membership without the common currency can be maintained. It is currently something of a paradox that while public opinion has become more pro-European, political disputes between parties are more structured along Eurosceptic lines.

In the aftermath of the Brexit referendum, there were discussions about a possible domino-effect which never materialised. Instead, there appeared to be increased appetite for further integration. The limited articulation of Swedish long-term strategic interests in the EU has increased the risks of marginalisation. This has become particularly pressing now as an important partner is set to leave the EU. Despite the nebulous debate on Europe in Sweden, efforts have been made to identify new strategies for how Sweden should re-orient its alliances within the EU after Brexit. To that end, both an intensified Nordic cooperation as well as stronger ties to bigger countries, in particular to Germany, have been mentioned as possible ways forward. However, the main possible trend of deepened cooperation within the eurozone and its implications for EU27 have mainly been superficially addressed in wider political debates.

In relation to the more long-term consequences of Brexit and the future development of the EU, Sweden should engage itself more actively in EU-affairs both at home and in interactions with others. The ability to analyse and assess tendencies should be further strengthened to become a proactive party in these discussions. In terms of alliances one should support, it is important to seek close collaboration with member countries that are perceived to be close to Sweden, such as the other Nordic countries or the Netherlands. This should not, however, stand in the way of seeking broader and/or unorthodox fora for exchanging ideas and reflection. In discussions about the future of the EU, it is especially important for smaller member states to be clear about which policy areas need more integration and those where national self-determination is seen as especially valuable. It is also important to have well-founded assessments and preferences on future institutional developments, including in areas where a non-eurozone member is not directly involved. Good preparation and anchoring at home will strengthen the capacity to exert influence at the European level.

Sweden should also endeavour to broaden and safeguard its relations with member states and to be more active in terms of its interactions with supranational institutions. It appears probable that the large member states, especially Germany, will have a central role in the EU in the future. At the same time, it is worth mentioning that forms of collaboration need to vary between different areas and on different occasions. Equally, as the future EU will consist of 27 member states, a number of relationships should be maintained while new ones should be built. It is at the same time important to connect long-term issues and priorities with more short-term issues, such as migration policy, where Sweden holds a strong and somewhat notable position. It is important to establish functioning systems to create these priorities and make them operational.

The typical Swedish response in all discussions about the future of the EU since it became a member has been to maintain the status quo. Considering the challenges facing the EU today combined with the changes already underway, this seems to be – more than ever – a rather insufficient standpoint. Regardless of the preferences about what kind of EU one wants, there should at least be a more active and nuanced public debate in Sweden about the future of the EU. Power and democracy are no longer issues that can be debated exclusively from a domestic political perspective.

Towards a "Reset" of EU-Swiss Relations?

Frank Schimmelfennig

Switzerland is a non-member state without membership aspirations. In fact, less than one in five Swiss have been in favour of EU membership in recent years. Switzerland's stake in the future of the European project is thus generally limited to managing and developing "bilateralism" – its unique relationship with the EU. At the same time, the politics of EU-Swiss relations are typical of the difficulties of non-members (and the exiting UK) in finding a viable relationship with the EU within the constraints of domestic Euroscepticism and international economic interdependence.

Bilateralism consists of a dense network of issue-specific intergovernmental treaties providing for selective mutual market access and sectoral cooperation. Bilateralism finds general public support in Switzerland, but it is vulnerable to repeated attacks by Switzerland's biggest party, the Swiss People's Party (SVP), to popular initiatives and referendums and to its complex and unsettled institutional setup.

Switzerland's relationship to the EU has gone through a particularly difficult period after Swiss voters narrowly accepted the "Mass Immigration Initiative" (MII) in February 2014. The MII confirmed that, in spite of being a non-member state, Switzerland is firmly embedded in the politics

F. Schimmelfennig (✉)
Centre for Comparative and International Studies, Swiss Federal Institute of Technology (ETH), Zurich, Switzerland
e-mail: frank.schimmelfennig@eup.gess.ethz.ch

M. Kaeding et al. (eds.), *The Future of Europe*,
https://doi.org/10.1007/978-3-319-93046-6_30

of European integration – and under the same populist pressures as member states. The vote mandated the Swiss government to negotiate and implement restrictions to the free movement of labour, what the EU point of view deems to be an "indispensable" pillar of bilateralism. In response, the EU cancelled Switzerland's association to EU research funding and student exchange programmes and put several additional sectoral agreements on hold. Most importantly, it plainly refused to enter into negotiations but threatened Switzerland with ending bilateral treaties on market access, which are legally linked to the freedom of movement.

Seeing how rigidly the EU defended the integrity of the Single Market, the Swiss Federal Council resigned itself to an extremely light implementation of the MII that would remain within the legal boundaries of its treaties with the EU. Even though its implementation fundamentally deviated from the text of the Initiative, referendum attempts against the government's implementation measures did not get off the ground.

Experiencing the EU's resolve and the high economic price of restricting the freedom of movement, Switzerland has gone through a learning process that has only just started in the UK. The fact that the Swiss government had sufficient room to manoeuvre facilitated the implementation of a pragmatic solution. As anti-EU hardliners in the SVP and the allied Action for an Independent and Neutral Switzerland (AUNS) are launching an even more radical anti-free movement initiative, the durability of the MII lesson remains to be seen.

For now, Swiss-EU relations are on a path to renormalisation. In January 2017, Switzerland's agreement on the freedom of movement with Croatia, the EU's most recent member state, entered into force. In return, Switzerland regained its associate member status in European research cooperation. In November 2017, Switzerland released the "Eastern billion", which contributes to projects with Eastern European member states. In a parallel movement, the EU unblocked negotiations on other issues such as Swiss participation in the EU emissions trading scheme, Swiss access to the Eurodac fingerprint database, and the revision of the Swiss-EU bilateral agreement on insurances.

That leaves one major obstacle: the institutional framework of Swiss-EU relations. Bilateralism follows the principles of static international agreements and diplomatic dispute settlement. Substantive policy rules in bilateral agreements largely mirror EU rules at the time of negotiation. Whenever EU rules change, however, bilateral rules need to be negotiated and adopted separately in EU-Swiss joint committees (or, alternatively, through unilateral adoption in Swiss legislation). Both options create legal uncertainty. Moreover, bilateralism has no judicial mechanism for monitoring compliance, interpreting the rules, and settling disputes.

The EU therefore proposes to shift to "dynamic adaptation" as a general principle known from the European Economic Area and applied in Switzerland's Schengen membership. Switzerland accepts a dynamic but refuses an "automatic" adaptation. Rather, the adaptation of EU law would remain subject to the full range of national procedures, including referendums. Moreover, the EU insists on judicial monitoring and enforcement, which is ultimately based on the EU Court of Justice. By contrast, the Swiss negotiation mandate envisages that the EU and Switzerland monitor compliance in their respective territories. It accepts the authority of the EU Court for the interpretation of the bilateral law but only accords it a consultative role in dispute settlement. Generally, the Swiss position is driven by the preservation of formal Swiss sovereignty and the desire to retain the ultimate control over binding rules, their monitoring, and adjudication. Especially "foreign judges", i.e. the EU Court, is a toxic concept in Swiss public discourse.

Negotiations on a new institutional framework have been going on since May 2014 and have reached a dead end. The EU rejects the negotiation of any new bilateral agreements unless the institutional issues are resolved. The new Swiss foreign minister Ignazio Cassis has vowed to hit the "reset" button; it is unclear, however, what this entails. Renaming the institutional framework agreement as a "friendship agreement", as proposed by Commission President Juncker in November 2017, will hardly do the trick.

At any rate, Swiss-EU relations are going to be a friendship with constant tugging, pinpricks, and missed opportunities unless the institutional issues are settled. In its current form, bilateralism is becoming ill suited for efficiently managing an increasingly intense and complex relationship between two highly interdependent polities and markets. As a tailor-made solution, bilateralism has served Switzerland well. It is, however, not a model for the future of the EU's economic relations with European non-member states – the UK or others.

Like a Candle in the Wind? Insights and Recommendations on the Turkish Accession to the EU

Başak Alpan

State of Play

"Europe" has been the most popular yet most volatile buzzword in Turkish politics for decades. It gained a particular momentum with the 1963 Ankara Agreement and then in 1999 during and after the Helsinki European Council when Turkey was officially accepted as an EU candidate. As a part of the pre-accession strategy, the Turkish government engaged in a substantial reform wave between 1999 and 2005 and amended almost 51 articles of the Constitution in order to meet the EU's concerns with Turkish democracy. After opening accession negotiations on October 3, 2005, we have seen a decrease in the intensity of the reforms; i.e. "reform fatigue". After 2005, "Europe" has no longer emerged as the *lingua franca* in Turkey.

The EU's waning image as an anchor of democratisation became all the more apparent in the July 2007 and June 2011 parliamentary elections,

B. Alpan (✉)
Centre for European Studies, Middle East Technical University, Ankara, Turkey
e-mail: balpan@metu.edu.tr

M. Kaeding et al. (eds.), *The Future of Europe*,
https://doi.org/10.1007/978-3-319-93046-6_31

where the AKP won around 49% of the votes each year. Therefore, AKP felt no urgency for the EU's democratization agenda anymore. This shift was also coupled with governmental and public disenchantment with the EU.

In the evening of July 15, 2016, Turkey was shaken to its core by an unexpected coup d'état attempt. Subsequently, a state of emergency was declared, and tens of thousands were imprisoned and investigated for their alleged links to the coup. Subsequently, a constitutional referendum was held in April 2017, which granted President Erdoğan sweeping presidential powers. The EU's reaction to both events has been quite ambivalent. EU officials expressed their "full support to the democratically elected institutions of the country", while they diplomatically suggested that respect for human rights should be upheld.

Under these dire conditions, the current negotiation process between Turkey and the EU is not going well. 16 chapters out of 35 are currently open and 14 chapters are frozen due to vetoes from the Republic of Cyprus, France, and the European Council.

Policy Recommendations

1. **A holistic approach to Turkish accession should be pursued:** The years 2004 and 2005 witnessed fierce debates in Europe about Turkey's EU membership. Up until the very last minute before opening accession negotiations, Austria stated that the goal of accession negotiations should not be full membership. In a letter to the EU's conservative heads of government, Christian Democrat leader Angela Merkel said negotiations with Turkey should not automatically lead to membership (a month before her party won in Germany's elections). They recommend instead that negotiations should be "open ended" and should lead to a "privileged partnership". From this time on, Turkey began to argue that the EU was not really serious about Turkey's accession bid. Regardless of the reforms Turkey fulfilled, its membership would be vetoed. Alternative integration scenarios such as "privileged partnership" add to the country's disenchantment with the EU. The re-emergence of these scenarios would remind the country of its skeletons in the closet, which the Turkish public and politicians do not particularly like. Similarly, sector-based integration with Turkey (in areas of energy, defence, or trade) should not be seen as an alternative to full membership. The EU should not give up insisting on democratisation and the accession process.

2. **Chapters 23 and 24 should be opened immediately:** In 2012, as a part of the 2011 Enlargement Strategy, the Commission amended its enlargement strategy by prioritizing rule of law and judicial reform, which meant that all accession negotiations would commence with these two chapters. However, since Cyprus vetoed the decision to open Chapters 23 (Judiciary and Fundamental Rights) and 24 (Justice, Freedom, and Society), the new strategy could not be implemented in Turkey. Progress Reports on Turkey have consistently criticised the lack of impartiality in the judiciary and the rule of law. Blocking the chapters that would potentially lead to an amelioration of points of criticism raised by the EU is a joke and should be dealt with at a diplomatic level within the EU.
3. **Communication as well as conditionality:** The EU might be right with its criticisms about the current state of democracy and human rights in Turkey, and the country might be reacting too much. Nevertheless, EU member states are not totally innocent in terms of their ambivalent attitudes vis-a-vis Turkey for some 60 years since the Ankara Agreement. We already know that the negotiation process is not a purely technical one, and Turkey is currently not the most favourite EU candidate. There are things that we cannot change as ordinary citizens or scholars (such as the non-recognition of the Republic of Cyprus or the Turkey-Russia rapprochement), but there are things we could change, like keeping the channels of communication between Turkish and European publics open. What really matters is communication between the two sides, alongside conditionality. It will be the people, especially the younger generations, who can change the existing status quo of stigmatised and protracted political problems between Turkey and the EU. The EU must support the formal (lobbying activities) and informal (civil society initiatives) ties between Turkey and the EU, just as it had promised to do in 2011 under the rubric of the Positive Agenda.
4. **Europe needs to tackle its own problems:** The future of EU-Turkey relations is about the EU as much as it is about Turkey. It is not a well-kept secret that the European project is in perpetual crisis. It would be naive not to recognise the shifting mood in Europe, encompassed by the rise of nationalism, populism, and a nation-first agenda, as well as a growing resistance to globalisation and immigration against the background of economic turbulences following the 2008 global financial crisis.

On March 25, 2017, EU leaders came together in Rome to celebrate the 60th anniversary of the Treaties of Rome by reflecting on past achievements and debating about how the shared European future would look like. What is really needed is a creative rejuvenation of the entire European project that can face global and regional challenges.

The Union after Brexit: Disintegration, Differentiation or Deepening?

Brendan Donnelly

Given that the United Kingdom now appears on course to leave the European Union in March 2019, there is little expectation that British preferences or concerns will play any direct role in the future evolution of the Union. For a number of years, British policy towards the European Union had anyway largely consisted of the search for ever more exceptions and opt-outs, leaving others, particularly the members of the eurozone, to direct the broader evolution of the Union.

British public and political opinion is, however, concerned with the intractable question of the nature of the UK's future relationship with the EU, especially its trading relationship. This question divides Mrs. May's Conservative Party in particular between those who wish, even after Brexit, to remain economically close to and aligned with the European Union and those who seek a different economic model along non-European lines. The Prime Minister knows that the adoption of either of these options has the potential to destroy the internal stability of the governing party. Like many in her Party, Mrs. May simply wishes to combine all the perceived advantages of membership in the EU with none of the perceived disadvantages.

B. Donnelly (✉)
Federal Trust for Education and Research, London, UK
e-mail: brendan.donnelly@fedtrust.co.uk

M. Kaeding et al. (eds.), *The Future of Europe*,
https://doi.org/10.1007/978-3-319-93046-6_32

That aspiration is wholly unrealistic. When Mrs. May and her party finally make a choice, it will inevitably be a painful one. It would be economically less disruptive for the UK to remain in the European Single Market and Customs Union after Brexit. However, it makes little political sense to leave the European Union only to remain bound by most of its rules and regulations with no say in their formulation. This in essence is the logically irresolvable conundrum created by the result of the referendum on June 23, 2016.

To the extent that the future development of the Union without the United Kingdom remains a matter of some interest on this side of the English Channel, three general approaches can be discerned: one predicts the imminent demise of the European Union; another foresees a more disparate and differentiated Union; and a third expects a notable acceleration in the pace of European integration after Brexit. These approaches often reflect the conscious or unconscious preferences of those holding them.

Most of those in the UK who continue to envisage the rapid collapse of the European Union hoped and believed that the British referendum of June 2016 would provide the starting-point for a series of political and electoral victories in mainland Europe won by parties hostile to the European Union. Many of those British electors who voted to leave the European Union had, for many years, been subjected by their newspapers and favourite television programmes to an unremitting presentation of the European Union as fundamentally corrupt, oppressive, incompetent, and divided. For such electors, voting to leave the Union in the EU referendum was not merely the right decision for the United Kingdom, but it was also the right decision for Europe as a whole.

An alternative British analysis, prevalent particularly among a section of those who voted "remain" in 2016, is that while Brexit will not be the precursor of a general dissolution of the European Union, the circumstances leading up to it demonstrate the unavoidable necessity for the European Union to loosen its internal structures. Since the British referendum, tensions within the Union on such issues as asylum-seekers, the protection of human rights, and relations with Russia have noticeably increased. Perhaps, as these British commentators argue, the British referendum result was a "canary in the mine" for the European Union and drew attention to the dangers of an over-ambitious attempt by the Union to bind diverse economies and societies, such as Slovakia and Spain or

Belgium and Hungary, tightly together. In its own interest, the European Union needs to recognize that not all its members will be prepared to accept the degree of sovereignty-pooling implicit in the goal of an "ever closer union" in the long term. It might even be that the United Kingdom could re-enter a more differentiated European Union in due course in which the hitherto vague concept of "variable geometry" found more systematic institutional expression.

Finally, there are those in the United Kingdom who fear or hope that Brexit may be the occasion for a major shift in the quality of European integration, probably based around the eurozone. It was always a widespread view in Britain that the single European currency would inevitably require more political integration than its original institutional structures envisaged. Some commentators saw this as a reason why the UK could and should never join the euro. Others saw this as a reason why the UK should join the euro precisely in order to ensure that the single currency did not become the nucleus of a political construction hostile to British economic and political interests. It is undeniable that the crisis of the single European currency in 2008 and its only imperfect resolution since have undermined the prestige of the Union in the UK even among commentators not fundamentally hostile to the EU. Many such commentators hope and believe that it will be easier for the members of the eurozone to pursue that measure of political integration necessary to stabilize the single European currency for the longer term after Brexit. The election of Mr. Macron and his radical proposals for the reform of the eurozone have been of great interest and encouragement in this.

It is a temptation common to all countries of the European Union to regard the possible or desirable future evolution of the Union exclusively from a national perspective. The UK often gives way to this temptation. In reality, the European Union will not collapse because the United Kingdom has left it. The British desire to enjoy an exceptional status within the European Union is not widely shared in other countries, either at the political or public level. In reality, the question of whether the eurozone countries will need or wish to deepen their political integration is no more or less delicate or pressing as a result of the UK's decision to leave the European Union. In all the British analyses cited above, it is the common unspoken assumption that Brexit will be an important event not just for the UK but for the European Union as a whole. It may be an assumption owing more to British amour propre than to objective circumstances.

Index

A
Accession, xii, 13, 14, 49, 53, 54, 58, 69, 70, 95, 99, 101, 105, 121–124
Africa, vii, 95
Alliance, xii, xiii, 2, 41, 46, 53–55, 82, 98, 100, 110, 114
Arctic Council, 55
Asylum, vii, 35, 37, 103
Austria, xii, 1–3, 11, 103, 105, 122

B
Bailout, 95
Balkan, 9, 10, 14, 15, 46, 86
Banking Union, 26, 27, 47, 59, 63, 66, 82, 94, 95, 111
Belgium, xi, 5–8, 39, 73, 127
Border, vi, x, xii, 2, 6, 10, 11, 14, 23, 35, 47, 63, 74, 79, 86, 105, 106, 111
Brexit, 5–7, 10, 11, 25, 26, 28, 34, 35, 41, 42, 46, 54, 58, 63, 83, 84, 86, 110, 114, 125–127
Brussels, 6, 38, 49, 93, 97–99, 105, 107, 110
Bulgaria, x, xii, 9–11, 75, 99, 103

C
Capital, xiii, 3, 49, 67, 70
Capital market, v
CEE, *see* Central and Eastern Europe
Central and Eastern Europe (CEE), xi, 13–15, 49, 91, 99, 103
CETA, 1, 6
China, vi, 9, 44
Citizens, vi, vii, ix, xiii, 6, 17, 20, 23, 30, 59, 73, 75, 86, 87, 91, 98, 101, 102, 105, 109, 123
Climate change, vi, 111
Cohesion policy, v, 95
Convergence, vi, 40, 42, 46, 65, 66, 69, 70, 109
Cooperation, x, 2, 3, 7, 15, 34, 35, 50, 53, 55, 58–60, 71, 78, 79, 86, 91, 103, 107, 110, 111, 113, 114, 117, 118

M. Kaeding et al. (eds.), *The Future of Europe*,
https://doi.org/10.1007/978-3-319-93046-6

Core, xi, xii, 1, 9, 15, 19, 22, 26, 27, 37, 42, 59, 60, 65, 71, 77–79, 95, 104, 122
Council of Ministers, 75
Court of Justice, 42, 119
Crisis/Crises, ix, 5, 7, 10, 11, 13, 18, 19, 21, 22, 27, 31, 33–35, 38, 42, 43, 45, 46, 59, 61, 62, 73–75, 77, 81, 89, 93, 102, 105, 106, 109–111, 114, 123, 127
Criticism, xii, 78, 84, 90, 123
Croatia, xii, 13–15, 103, 106, 118
Currency, vi, vii, 6, 35, 42, 73, 91, 94, 113, 114, 127
Cyprus, 17–20, 47, 122, 123
Czech Republic, xii, 21–24

D
Debate, vii, ix–xiii, 2, 3, 5–7, 11, 15, 17–19, 33, 35, 38, 39, 41, 43, 45, 46, 54, 55, 58, 59, 64, 70, 71, 81, 83, 84, 86, 89, 93, 94, 98, 104, 114, 115, 122
Debt, vi, 39, 47, 63, 94, 111
Deepen, x, xii, xiii, 7, 34, 40, 47, 59, 65–67, 84, 114, 127
Defence, vi, x, 2, 6, 7, 11, 34, 35, 37, 55, 58, 59, 71, 79, 83, 94, 109, 111, 122
Democracy, vii, 9, 43, 50, 64, 90, 97–100, 109, 115, 121, 123
Denmark, xii, 25–28
Digital market, v, 75
Diplomacy, vii, 111
Diversity, ix, x, 7, 38, 73–76
Domestic, xii, 9–11, 13, 22–24, 38, 51, 61, 62, 78, 90, 102, 109, 111, 115, 117
Dublin, xi

E
Economic and Monetary Union (EMU), 42, 47, 58, 59, 61–63, 65–67, 73, 74, 82, 93–95, 114
EEA, *see* European Economic Area
EFSF, *see* European Financial Stability Facility
EFSI, *see* European Fund for Strategic Investments
EFTA, *see* European Free Trade Association
e-governance, 29
Election, x, 6, 11, 27, 37, 41, 49, 51, 58, 62–64, 78, 102, 121, 122, 127
EMF, *see* European Monetary Fund
Emigration, xi, 13, 67, 70
EMU, *see* Economic and Monetary Union
Energy, 2, 6, 19, 55, 66, 69, 99, 111, 122
Energy market, v
Enlargement, xiii, 2, 3, 14, 15, 22, 54, 74, 82, 99, 107, 110, 114, 123
Environment, x, xii, 34, 42, 46–47, 87
ESM, *see* European Stability Mechanism
Estonia, xi, 29–31
EU, *see* European Union
EUREKA, 107
Euro, 8, 10, 14, 26, 27, 33, 34, 81, 83, 91, 109, 114, 127
Eurobarometer, 6, 18, 21, 34, 62, 70, 73, 101, 109
Eurogroup, 67, 75, 93, 94
Europe, v–vii, ix–xiii, 1–3, 7, 14, 15, 17–20, 25–28, 30, 34, 37–40, 42, 43, 45–47, 51, 54, 55, 58, 63, 66, 74, 77–79, 84–91, 93–95, 97, 111, 113, 114, 121–123, 126

European Border and Coast Guard Agency, vi
European Central Bank, 67
European Commission, ix, 17, 25, 31, 54, 58, 66, 83, 93, 97, 98
European Council, 67, 121, 122
European Economic Area (EEA), 33, 53–55, 119
European Financial Stability Facility (EFSF), 81
European Free Trade Association (EFTA), 53, 54
European Fund for Strategic Investments (EFSI), 81
European Monetary Fund (EMF), 42, 47, 63, 82
European Parliament, vi, vii, x, 2, 29, 41, 67, 75, 78, 82, 102
European Stability Mechanism (ESM), 42, 47, 63, 67, 81
European Union (EU), ix, xi, 1, 3, 5–9, 13–15, 17, 21, 25, 29, 30, 33–37, 41–44, 46, 49, 53, 57–67, 69–71, 73–78, 86, 89, 93, 97–101, 105, 109–111, 113–115, 117–119, 121–127
Eurosceptic, x, 6, 18, 21–24, 34, 61, 81, 83, 84, 103, 109, 114
Eurozone, xii, 11, 15, 18, 21, 26, 27, 33, 37–39, 42, 46, 47, 63, 64, 66, 69–71, 74, 75, 78, 82, 84, 94, 95, 113, 114, 125, 127
Eurozone budget, 42, 47

F
Finance minister, 37, 42, 47, 63, 75, 76
Finland, x, 33–36
Foreign policy, vi, 13, 22, 34, 35, 47, 54, 59, 65, 94, 95, 109, 111
France, xi, 3, 11, 19, 34, 37–40, 42, 46, 74, 84, 110, 111, 122
Free movement, 1, 54, 67, 73, 118
FRONTEX, 47
Future of Europe, vii, ix, x, xiii, 2, 3, 7, 45–48, 54, 55, 59, 87, 88, 93, 94, 100, 102, 104

G
GDP, 23, 46, 47, 67, 70, 71
Germany, 2, 3, 11, 13, 37, 38, 40–44, 54, 55, 71, 73, 84, 87, 110, 114, 115, 122
Governance, vi, 14, 35, 82, 109, 114
Greece, x, 13, 19, 43, 45–48, 103
Growth, vi, xi, 3, 34, 46, 62, 77, 78, 94, 95, 98

H
Heads of State and Government, vii, ix
High Representative, 67
Hungary, xi, 10, 22, 49–51, 90, 127

I
Iceland, x, xiii, 33, 53–55, 86
Identity, vii, xi, 2, 19, 29, 54, 90, 91
Illiberal, 50, 90
Immigration, vi, vii, 62, 111, 123
India, vi
Innovation, vi, xi, 35
Institution, vi, ix, 10, 11, 18, 20, 27, 31, 38, 39, 42, 49, 50, 54, 55, 59, 62, 66, 67, 74, 78, 79, 83, 90, 91, 95, 110, 111, 115, 122
Integration, ix–xiii, 1–3, 5–8, 10, 11, 14, 15, 18, 21, 22, 26, 33, 34, 38, 40, 42, 44, 46, 47, 50, 51, 57–60, 63, 65, 67, 69, 71, 74, 75, 82–84, 86, 89–91, 94, 95, 97, 99, 101, 103, 104, 111, 114, 115, 118, 122, 126, 127

Investment, vi, 44, 63, 71, 79, 82, 94, 99
Ireland, xi, 13, 57–60, 70, 76
Italy, x, 19, 43, 47, 61–64, 78, 84, 110

J
Jobs, v, vi, 3, 13, 18, 37–40, 110
Juncker, Jean-Claude, vii, ix, 63, 75, 81, 82, 84, 97, 106, 119

L
Latvia, xi, 65–67
Lithuania, xi, 69–71, 103
Luxembourg, xi, 73–76

M
Maastricht Treaty, 26, 61
Macron, Emmanuel, vii, ix–xi, 25, 26, 28, 37–39, 41, 42, 44, 45, 81, 82, 84, 86, 127
Malta, x, 77–79
Market, vi, vii, 3, 6, 23, 35, 39, 42–43, 59, 67, 87, 89, 113, 117–119
Mass Immigration Initiative (MII), 117, 118
Mediterranean, 46, 58, 77–79, 89, 110
Membership, xii, 1–3, 6, 11, 18, 19, 33, 53, 54, 57, 65, 69, 70, 74, 77–78, 86, 90, 91, 95, 101–105, 107, 117, 119, 122, 125
Merkel, Angela, 42–44, 50, 86, 122
MFF, *see* Multiannual Financial Framework
MII, *see* Mass Immigration Initiative
Multiannual Financial Framework (MFF), ix, 41, 111
Multispeed, xi, 7, 15, 26, 63, 66, 74, 87, 97

N
National, 1, 2, 6, 10, 11, 19, 35, 39, 42, 58–60, 66, 67, 76, 79, 90, 94, 102, 103, 111, 127
Nationalist, 6, 7, 22, 63, 98, 110
NATO, 34, 49, 51, 55, 58, 70, 71, 78, 79, 87, 105
Netherlands, 11, 46, 81–84, 111, 114
Norms, xi, 40, 50, 51, 67
Norway, x, xiii, 33, 55, 85–88

O
Opt-out, xii, 26, 27, 33, 75, 125
Orbán, Viktor, 22, 26, 43, 49–51

P
Periphery, x, xii, 27, 28, 59, 78, 102, 113–115
PESCO, 26, 58, 95
Poland, xi, 10, 22, 49–51, 70, 89–91, 98, 103, 110
Policies, vi, ix, x, xii, 1, 2, 6–8, 15, 22, 33, 35–38, 40–44, 46, 54, 55, 58, 59, 62, 63, 66, 67, 69–71, 73–75, 78, 79, 82, 84, 89, 94, 95, 103, 106, 107, 109–111, 115, 118, 122–125
Populism, xii, 9, 10, 93, 123
Portugal, xii, 93–95, 110
Prosperity, vii

R
Referendum, 23, 27, 58, 63, 77, 105, 114, 117–119, 122, 126
Reform, vi, ix, 3, 6, 10, 11, 35, 36, 38, 42, 46, 59, 61–64, 69–71, 82, 84–86, 97, 99, 105, 121–123, 127

Refugee, 2, 3, 10, 14, 27, 43, 46–48, 51, 74, 75, 89, 90, 93, 103, 105, 111
Relationship, xi, xiii, 55, 58, 61–64, 85–87, 115, 117, 119, 125
Rhetoric, xi, 90, 98, 104
Romania, xii, 9, 75, 97–100, 103
Russia, vi, 9, 34, 35, 44, 54, 66, 70, 89, 126

S
Scenario, vii, ix, 7, 9, 19, 74, 93, 94, 97, 100, 122
Schengen, xii, 14, 15, 54, 55, 63, 69, 75, 78, 95, 119
SDG, *see* Sustainable Development Goal
Security, x, 2, 6, 18, 19, 30, 33–36, 46, 55, 59, 69–71, 78, 79, 81, 89, 94, 99, 107
Single market, 13, 23, 26, 65–67, 86, 94, 118
Slovakia, 101–104, 126
Slovenia, xii, 14, 105–107
Social Pillar, xi, 74, 76
Social Union, 2, 66–67
Solidarity, x, 10, 11, 18, 23, 34, 42, 43, 59, 67, 74, 75, 78, 89–91, 95, 101, 103
Sovereignty, vi, x, 1, 28, 58, 67, 71, 74, 90, 113, 119
Spain, xii, 109–111, 126
Spitzenkandidaten, 82
Stability and Growth Pact, vi, 62
Sustainable Development Goal (SDG), 87
Sweden, xii, 35, 70, 111, 113–115
Switzerland, x, xiii, 86, 117–119

T
Tajani, Antonio, vii
Tax evasion, 3, 23
Tax harmonisation, 71, 78, 79
Technology, vi, 29, 30, 111
Terrorism, vi, 19, 34, 111
Trade, v, vi, xii, 1, 6, 23, 40, 66, 122
TTIP, 1, 6
Turkey, x, xiii, 2, 9, 10, 48, 86, 121–123

U
Ukraine, 34, 70, 86
Unemployment, xi, 1, 21, 39, 62, 67, 77, 106
Union, v–vii, x, xii, xiii, 1–3, 8, 9, 11, 17–20, 34, 46, 47, 55, 57, 65, 74, 78, 79, 97, 113, 125–127
United Kingdom (UK), xi, xiii, 7, 25, 28, 34, 58, 59, 70, 78, 83, 86, 87, 113, 114, 117–119, 125–127
United States (USA), vi, 39, 58, 71, 75, 99

V
Value, v, vi, xi, xii, 3, 20, 22, 35, 44, 50, 51, 57, 71, 78, 87, 89–91, 95
Visegrád, 10, 23, 63, 64, 91

W
White Paper, vii, 17, 19, 93

Druck:
Customized Business Services GmbH
im Auftrag der
KNV Zeitfracht GmbH
Ein Unternehmen der Zeitfracht - Gruppe
Ferdinand-Jühlke-Str. 7
99095 Erfurt